T0208818

REVISITING THE MEMORIES OF YESTERDAY

LOOKING BACK

GEORGE E. SAURMAN

REVISITING THE MEMORIES OF YESTERDAY
LOOKING BACK

iUniverse books may be ordered through booksellers or by contacting:

iUniverse
1663 Liberty Drive
Bloomington, IN 47403
www.iuniverse.com
1-800-Authors (1-800-288-4677)

ISBN: 978-1-5320-1833-6 (sc)
ISBN: 978-1-5320-1834-3 (e)

Library of Congress Control Number: 2017903120

Print information available on the last page.

iUniverse rev. date: 03/24/2017

CONTENTS

DEDICATION

This book Is dedicated to Fort Washington Estates, an ACTS-Retirement-Life Community, in appreciation of the manner in which they provided a loving environment for the closing years of my life, beginning in March of the year 2001 when my wife, Mary, and I took up residence in their facility.

We had determined that the time had come when we should look for a less complicated life style. Cooking and cleaning for Mary had become a burden and I found house maintenance and lawn mowing a chore. We left our three story house and moved into an apartment, placing our lives in the hands of the people at Fort Washington Estates and we never once looked back or felt a moment of reluctance.

A great load had been taken off of our backs and we discovered a new freedom, having escaped from many of the daily responsibilities which had begun to weigh heavily on our daily lives. We were free to take trips with no concern for what might happen to our home while we were away. Just pack and get in the car and go.

The dedicated staff at Fort Washington assumed all of those responsibilities. They also provided a daily source of multi-choice menus of delicious meals. We never left the table hungry or dissatisfied. We were free to join in the wide selection of activities or just remain to ourselves. The residents are wonderful.

When Mary began to have health problems we were supported by well trained, caring nurses. Her passing in 2012 was difficult to bear, but it was because of losing her, not for want of help, nor lack of sympathy. I could not have asked for any greater care for her.

So while documenting some of the memories of yesterday, my experience as a resident at Fort Washington Estates ranks near the top.

PREFACE

Storytelling takes many forms. It can be oral or in written form. In any event, it is intended to entertain and often educate. In this work I attempted to narrate those parts of a very full and productive life that have proven of interest to listeners who have suggested that it should be put in writing for others to enjoy.

As a medium to illustrate how rapidly things have changed, it is amazing how many aspects of life have experienced transition over the last hundred years, but perhaps even more amazing as we look about us and witness the ongoing onslaught of technological discoveries that come on the market. The days of the pony express are gone forever but the advent of new forms of communication and many medical discoveries is breathtaking. In the midst of all the change, God remains the same today as when He created the earth and established His laws of nature. Man does not modify them, he can only work around them. His work has no expiration date until He blows the whistle.

INTRODUCTION

Conversation is a major focal point among retired people. Most have put aside many of the more physical activities of life, but the mind continues to journey on. Current events, reflecting on the past and looking ahead to future happenings all play a role in the conscious considerations of the mind.

Since experience creates the substance of memory and helps direct future planning, the diversity of the population at Fort Washington becomes a valuable resource which fuels both one's increased understanding and his personal recall of past events. The process is fascinating for that which took place long ago has many ramifications for all of us today.

I have included the biographies of several of my fellow residents at the conclusion of my own story in order to share that diversity.

IN THE BEGINNING

As I look out the window I see snowflakes falling from the sky. Already they have covered the ground with an accumulation of about three inches and it looks as though much more is coming. One of the things that occurs to me is that throughout my ninety-one years, the reality of snowflakes falling from the sky has remained unchanged.

Since my purpose is to reflect upon the multitude of things that have changed over those years, it is not just coincidental that things such as snow, rain, sunshine, daylight and nightfall continue to occur with a certainty that provides the consistency and predictability that accompanies God's creation. Everything related to God and his miraculous establishment of life itself, the earth, and the conditions that have existed on a regular basis from the beginning of time, has remained unchanged. That being said, what man has done within those predictable circumstances has been an ongoing evolution of vast dimension.

What we have achieved in order to improve the conditions under which we live has been equally miraculous. It is my personal belief that God unfolds to mankind some of His secrets over time which enables us to improve our circumstances. He has also equipped us with a brain with which to deliberate on how to improve our lot. It is on those changes that I intend to focus in this book because, on reflection, there have been a great many of them and to those persons of more recent generations it is interesting to see how we were able to cope with some of the challenges facing us as we grew up. Indeed, while God and His creation remain dependable and fixed, mankind has altered his response to the conditions in which he finds himself in various ways for his own convenience and progress.

My story begins personally on January 15, 1926 when I was born to Marcelene Borst Saurman and Benjamin Franklin Saurman in a hospital in Houston, Texas. I inherited two sibling brothers, Richard and John Robert (Dick and Bob). Within a year the family was heading north to Baltimore. Because of my work on this book I wondered (for the first time ever) how we made the trip. I assume it was by automobile, certainly not by air or bus, because no such opportunity existed for us. Probably it was in a "Model T" Ford automobile because it would have been the least expensive means of transportation available.

The invention 0f the automobile is considered the most important development in the history of transportation since the discovery of the wheel. The automobile was not invented by a single person or in a single day. Rather it involved evolution in worldwide technology that transpired over centuries.

It was 1885 when Karl Benz built the first practical auto powered by an internal combustion engine. In 1898 Charles and Frank Duryea built an engine- driven carriage in Springfield, Massachusetts. Ransom Eli Olds was first to mass produce cars in Detroit and merged in 1908 with Buick to form General Motors.

From 1915-25 Henry Ford focused on decreasing the cost of automobiles and developed the Model T. It was popularly known as the "Tin Lizzie" because the body was made of sheet metal and "Lizzie" was a name commonly given to horses. It originally cost $850 but by 1927 it had been brought down to only $250. That made it cheap enough for my father to have gotten possession of one.

It required a crank to start the engine and the headlights were replaced by unscrewing the burned out bulb and replacing it with a new one. Mechanical brakes were employed to stop the car and a clutch allowed the changing of gears. It was a real challenge to operate, especially when compared with the ease of driving today. It was better than the horse and carriage and far superior to walking, especially with a family.

We didn't stay long in Baltimore, but made a rather permanent move to Pennsylvania where my mother's family lived. We lived in a row house at 212 Parker Avenue in a small area of Delaware County known as Highland Park. We were immersed in the depression and my father was out of work. My mother learned to do hairdressing and was supporting the family on what she earned. I have since taken my wife and children back to show them the house in which we had lived. It was hard even for me to have imagined just how narrow the house was and while we didn't go inside, I can remember the hot summer nights without air conditioning when I would lie in pools of perspiration in my third floor cot, and how hard it was to get to sleep.

Early efforts to develop some form of air conditioning dated back to 1830 when a doctor in Florida used an ice-making machine to blow cold air across his patients who suffered from yellow fever and malaria.

In 1925 the first movie theater offered air conditioning and it was a real treat to attend a theater equipped with air conditioning on a hot Saturday afternoon, even though it cost ten cents which cut into the money for penny candy. Extensive use of air conditioning exists today in homes and has become an expected necessity in hospitals, schools and office buildings.

In 1930 Frigidaire developed the first hydro chlorofluorocarbon refrigerant known as Freon. Safety and cost remained an obstacle to its widespread use, but today every home has replaced the old ice box with an electric refrigerator. Most of the folks in the retirement community in which I now reside remember hearing the lonesome cry of the ice man as he made his daily trip through each community with his horse drawn wagon loaded with huge cakes of ice. Some of the more courageous children would hop on the back of his wagon and grab a small piece of ice.

My mother and father were divorced while I was in the early years of my elementary education. She had learned the hairdressing trade and supported the family. My oldest brother, Dick, had fallen from a tree and punctured a lung. He missed a year of school and graduated the same year as my other brother, Bob (1940). My mother married Abe Quay and I now had a step-father. Financially things got a little better. Before I left junior high school and entered Upper Darby Senior High I had a half-brother, Harry Quay.

We moved several times within Upper Darby Township. My brother, Bob, used to say, "my folks moved about many times, but we always managed to find them." I recall visiting my mother's parents, Albert and Emina Hansell Borst, in Media, PA (Penna. in those days), where they lived on Orange Street. My grandfather was a Reader in the First Church of Christ Scientist and employed as an insurance adjuster. His personality was perfect for such a position. He was loved by all, and the women at church called him "Daddy Borst." He was my mentor and I always wanted to be just like him.

He taught me many things about how to live my life according to the Ten Commandments and the book of Proverbs. He also taught me the Golden Rule to treat others as you would have them treat you and the words to the following hymn which has served me well throughout my life:

> Shepherd, show me how to go.
> O'er the hillside steep,
> How to gather, how to sew,
> How to feed thy sheep.
> I will listen for thy voice,
> Lest my footsteps stray
> I will follow and rejoice
> All the rugged way.

There was a whip-like object that was used to clean carpets during spring cleaning at their Media home. The rugs were suspended from the clothes line and then a metal instrument that resembled a tennis racquet with a long handle was used to literally beat the dust and dirt from the carpets. Different materials used in making carpets today, along with the invention of the vacuum cleaner, have relegated this blister-creating instrument to the annals of antiquity, although it was years before we had one.

What We Did for fun

During the early years of my growing up there were many things which are mostly absent from the experiences of today's youth. Playing marbles was a big time pastime. Marbles were about half an inch in diameter and made of glass. They were beautifully colored. We would draw a circle in the dirt and place a number of marbles in the center. We would then take turns aiming at the pack with our "shooter" which was a larger marble and one that we prized greatly. We would keep any marbles that we succeeded in knocking out of the circle. When we missed, the next player took his turn. I don't remember ever playing marbles with a girl, but perhaps some girls did play.

Girls were mostly into jacks, a game which involved placing several metal objects that looked like plus signs on the floor and then tossing a rubber ball into the air and picking up the jacks, one at a time before the ball landed. They also played a game called hopscotch. To do this they had to draw a playing field on the sidewalk with a piece of chalk. It was like a huge "t" with several blocks about two feet square, adjoining each other, with a square on either side to form the "T" and then another block. The player would then throw a marker onto the field, hop to that item one square at a time, pick up the marker, and then complete the course, hopping all the way. The squares were numbered and the player advanced one number at a time until completing the course.

Another activity that we guys participated in was making and shooting rubber band guns at each other. The gun was made by taking a rectangular piece of wood about fifteen inches long, three inches wide and three-quarters of an inch thick. We attached a half of a clothes pin to one end of the wood by stretching a piece of inner tube about half an inch thick from one end of the gun to the other, encompassing the clothes pin. We then tucked one end of another rubber band into the space made by depressing the lower end of the clothes pin into the small space between it and the wood at the top,

By depressing the lower portion of the clothes pin, the rubber band was released and sailed through the air. There was an eight penny nail hammered into the bottom of the device as a trigger to hold onto when putting pressure on the lower end of the clothes pin. The rubber bands came from cutting a deflated inner tube from an automobile flat tire, usually red in color, into strips of about half an inch wide. These inner tubes are no longer found in automobile tires and at that time we had never heard of gun control. I never heard of anyone developing a criminal character as a result of our game playing, however.

Flat tires were not uncommon on automobiles in those days and when you had one, you had to take the jack from the trunk, jack up the car and remove the wheel, take out the deflated tube, replace it with a new one, inflate the tube with a tire pump, and replace the wheel. It was possible to place a patch over the hole, if you could locate it, and hold the patch in place with a special glue. Flat tires were never fun.

Our games were a bit more imaginative than many of their counter parts today. When we played baseball it was usually with a glove that had almost no padding or shape, a ball from which the cover had come off and had been replaced with tire tape and a broken bat that was a cast-off from one of the local adult teams which had broken. It was nailed together and taped over at the place where it was split. It usually stung your hands when you made contact with the ball. The field was full of ruts, and trophies for little league players were only for the for the Official Little League teams.

Our roller skates clamped onto the soles of our street shoes and frequently came off while skating. This really hurt when you were playing roller hockey in the streets where cinders often accumulated on the edges. Bruises and skinned knees were common.

In the evenings the neighborhood kids gathered on the corner and often played hide and seek or kick the can. Such rampant invasion onto neighborhood lawns and hiding in their back yards would cause 911 calls in today's insecure society.

I attended Highland Park Elementary School, the Junior High School and Upper Darby High School. I graduated in

1943 with honors. I had also been admitted to the National Honor Society, run Cross Country, served as Feature Editor of the newspaper and been awarded a full scholarship to Ursinus College. My divorced parents would never sign for me to play football because they feared that the other might sue them if I were injured playing. I was very satisfied with my high school education, an evaluation which I felt was confirmed when I was a student at Ursinus.

My brother, Dick, worked as a laundry route man, picking up and delivering clothes to be laundered and ironed. This too is a thing of the past because of the invention of electric clothes washers and spin dryers which were destined to replace the old ringer type dryers with which most of us were familiar.

He purchase a beautiful new 1939 Dodge sedan, of which he was extremely proud. It cost him a little over $800. He encouraged me on one occasion to get a date and accompany him and his date on a trip to Sunnybrook Ballroom, just outside of Pottstown, Pennsylvania, for a performance of Glen Miller and his band. It was so crowded that no one could dance and everyone just stood elbow to elbow, swaying back and forth to the music, packed in like sardines. One young lady up by the stage fainted and Glen Miller himself reached down from the stage to lift her up. Immediately she was joined by a couple more copycat fainters.

CHAPTER 2

AMERICA GOES TO WAR

On Dec. 7, 1941, the Japanese attacked our Naval Base at Pearl Harbor and at 4:10 PM Eastern Standard time, December 8th, President Franklin Delano Roosevelt declared war against Japan. Eleven days later Adolf Hitler declared war on the United States. We had become involved in a war of tremendous proportion, but It was a war that our entire nation unanimously supported. There was great pain and suffering for our men and women as they entered into a fight to the finish to save the world from a dictator determined to rule the world. Hitler's forces had already invaded one European nation after another, and was at that moment, threatening Great Britain. Japan had attacked our base at Pearl Harbor and our nation began a massive work effort to produce war equipment and ships in order to engage in the conflict; the government instituted the draft to establish fighting units.

As a nation we dedicated all of our resources, manpower and industries to the effort to meet the challenge. There was an amazing focus on enlarging our armed forces at every level, but we realized that this would not be sufficient to do the job. We also had to dedicate our total industrial resources to an extent that they had never before been tested. Women entered the work force in large numbers to replace the men who had been taken into the armed services. "Rosie the Riveter" became a familiar character. Shortages of certain materials, such as gasoline, butter, meat and sugar led to rationing.

We substituted margarine for butter. The early margarine was a white substance that was packaged in a plastic bag. Included was a small package with coloring in it. You had to mix the coloring into the bag of margarine and then squeeze and press the larger package until a fairly uniform pale orange color evolved. Greatly improved forms of margarine exist today which are used as a butter substitute because of a concern for calories, but in those days it was usually margarine or nothing.

In my family the war had some serious personal consequences. Gold stars began appearing in many windows indicating casualties from combat and my brother Dick was encountering a great deal of public pressure. Because of his lung problem he had been classified 4-F in the draft but outwardly he appeared perfectly healthy. Some of the mothers on his route caused him great concern because of remarks they made accusing him of being a draft dodger. He became so depressed that he had to seek other employment.

My Uncle, Bill Borst, was the CEO for Potts Ice Cream Company in Philadelphia and he hired him. Once again, challenged by the sting of being 4-F, he was showing off by unloading an ice cream freezer from a truck when the strain from lifting the freezer reopened the wound from his earlier fall. Had we had the medical equipment and medical skill of today, he would probably have survived this new set back, but he was unable to pull through and at the young age of 23, he passed on.

It was 1943, the year in which my other brother, Bob, serving with the 69th Infantry Division was taken prisoner in the attack on Anzio Beach, Italy. Remarkably my mother had a vision in which she saw Bob, helmetless and wondering about, but O.K. When Bob returned after the war, he verified the details of her vision. He had been rendered unconscious by a concussion grenade and when he regained consciousness, he was helmetless, dazed and taken prisoner by the Germans.

The family was notified that he was missing in action and it was quite a while before details of his being taken captive were related to us, but it was a relief to know that he had not been killed. My mother sent vitamins along with other goodies to him which he actually received, but the packages had been opened before they reached him. He later told us that he was fed as well as the German troops. The prison camp where he was held was located on a farm in Poland.

1943 was also the year that I graduated from high school. I was unable to take advantage of my scholarship to Ursinus College because my services were needed to help care for Dick. After he died, I started work as a sheet metal worker, second class, at Sun Shipbuilding Company in Chester, PA, building Liberty ships for transporting cargo and troops overseas. I worked the third shift, going in at 11 in the evening. It was quite an adjustment and altered my social life considerably.

I became an Air Raid Warden in my neighborhood with duties to look out for light shining from windows during black outs in air raid warning practice sessions. The law required all homes to be blacked out to prevent a potential target for enemy air planes and when the sirens blew, we took to the streets to look for violations.

Cooperation was almost perfect as people recognized the potential danger. There were reports of enemy submarines off the Atlantic shore with possible landings in the New England area. Ships were also being sunk off the coast. The war was physically closer than it might otherwise have seemed. No bombing attempts were ever reported to my knowledge, but the possibility was sufficient to cause people to exercise caution.

As the summer came to a close, I decided to enlist and entered the Army at the age of seventeen as a member of the Army Specialized Training Reserve Program and was sent to Carnegie Institute of Technology located in the city of Pittsburgh, PA. I completed my first semester and was made Cadet Commander of our training company, but on turning eighteen, I was transferred to New Cumberland near Harrisburg for assignment to basic Infantry training. The program originally called for my return to college following basic training, but money for the program was discontinued and I was in the Infantry for the duration of the war.

I was assigned to specialized training in communications which took place at Camp Blanding, Florida where I became a wire lineman, working with the installation of field telephones and switchboards. In addition to my infantry training I learned how to climb poles (or trees) with climbers strapped on my legs and a safety belt to be attached when I reached the desired height. The reason for climbing poles was to string the wire high enough to cross roads without being dislodged by truck traffic.

I also learned how to search out trouble on a telephone line. Sometimes it might be created as a result of the explosion of an artillery round or possibly by an enemy soldier deliberately cutting it. In any event, this was described as an "open" in the line and was relatively easy to locate by simply following the line and finding where it was separated.

More difficult to locate was a "short" in the line, resulting from bare wires being somehow crossed. The worst of these situations would usually be caused by an enemy inserting a pin through the wire causing the short. To locate a short, one had to use a field phone and make several calls to the switchboard. At the point where you could not get through, you would have just passed the short. Making repeated calls allowed you to pinpoint the short. This method in combat conditions involved possible danger because often the enemy would hide near the short and wait for the repairman. It was always good policy to make these ventures in pairs to provide protective cover.

Upon completing my training I was classified a Wire Lineman and transferred to Hattiesburg, Mississippi where the 65th Infantry Division was being formed for combat. However, they had already filled their requirement for wire linemen and I was assigned to a regular Infantry unit. Because of my size I was assigned to carry a Browning Automatic Rifle which used a magazine of twenty rounds. It was heavier in weight than a regular rifle and necessitated the carrying of considerably more ammunition, but it gave the squad more fire power. Our unit completed its training and we were ready to ship overseas. We were boarded onto a troop train and headed for Camp Kilmer, N.J.

My step-father and mother had decided to acquire a store which could provide employment in case either my brother or I became injured in combat. It was a small grocery store with an apartment on the second floor, located on the Delsea Drive in Franklinville, New Jersey. I was able to visit for a day and night before embarking on the troop ship heading overseas. The building was located next to a railroad track and during the night I was awakened when the house shook and a bright light filled my room. The sound of a steam engine roaring around the corner made me sit straight up in bed until I realized what was happening. It was good to get home to see the family. Harry had grown quite a bit and I had come to highly respect the role of my step-father. I was ready for what would come next.

The Trip Over

The trip across the Atlantic was without adventure, but we were never told where we were headed for security reasons. We marched aboard the ship and proceeded down into the hold where hundreds of bunks had been set up connected to upright poles rising from the bulkhead all the way to the upper deck. The bunks were supported by chains and were four high in number. I chose an upper bunk because I had had some experience on the water acquired during fishing trips with my family. I never got sick on those occasions, but I had seen others who were not so fortunate. It was just common sense to go to the top.

We were instructed to not go out on the deck at night. To encourage us to obey, we were told that a member of the crew had been washed overboard and we would not be able to go back to look for him. We learned when we were able to go out in the daylight that we were in a convoy. Ships surrounded us as far as one could see, with Navy ships including destroyers and cruisers providing a perimeter of security. It took us ten days to make the trip across the ocean because we were zigzagging to avoid submarines instead of taking a direct route.

Eating aboard ship can be a problem, especially in rough weather. We would line up next to a railing that would guide us along the chow line. Gleeful sailors enjoyed putting our food on our plates as we slid by. They call it "slinging the hash" and I must admit their aim was good for the most part, but at breakfast the eggs and oatmeal got better acquainted than I normally prefer.

The harbor at Le Harve, France had not been fully restored so the troop ship could not pull all the way in and we were taken ashore in small landing craft. It was January 22, 1945. We arrived in an encampment called Camp Lucky

Strike with many large tents, each of which accommodated a full infantry squad. The tents were snow covered and the area was in a state of partial completion as a result of the fact that the engineer battalion, which was in the process of setting it up, had been called to reinforce an area under siege in the Battle of the Bulge. A bit of exploration located two pot belly stoves which were welcome since it was cold and the wintry blasts were chilling.

Food and fuel were scarce. At one point spoons full of peanut butter were a treat, but gradually supplies began to catch up. This was to be our home until it was decided where we would be committed in combat. We trained regularly to be ready and with the cold wintry weather, the stoves came in handy. We also used them to hide food that we were able to scrounge, by digging a hole beneath them and supporting them with boards. One of our men spoke French fluently and he made evening trips into the nearby town with cigarettes to trade for bread, wine and other special delights.

It was not long before we moved by truck to a small town near Ennery which we learned was near the Siegfried Line of World War I. We learned also that we were a part of George Paton's Third Army. I volunteered to go on a series of patrols in order to get the experience of being under fire since we were a new and inexperienced outfit.

It was quite an experience and I think it did give me confidence when we actually headed into full scale combat. We were under the control of an Engineering Officer who narrated the objective of each of three special patrols, each more bizarre than the other. We would have to cross a stream in rubber rafts, make our way through the weeds on the other side and take a position along the trench through which the German guards would get into the concrete fortification. The goal was to "capture a Kraut."

There were five of us, the Lieutenant made six. We met in a deserted building on our side of the stream. The raft was waiting for us at the river's edge. We climbed aboard with three on each side and began to paddle into the darkness. Suddenly a flare lit up the sky. In training we were taught to freeze in such a situation. One side of the raft froze, the other paddled faster, causing the raft to turn in a circle. Fortunately the light was all that was involved and when we got the raft straightened out, we continued on toward the opposite shore.

When we touched land, the Lieutenant hoped out and told us to disembark but await further orders from him. He disappeared but returned in a moment or so and motioned for us to follow him. We had not gone far when the reeds under our feet were making a horrible noise and a machine gun to our front opened fire. He gave the command to return to the raft and we complied willingly. With determined strokes we made for the friendly shore and met briefly in the abandoned house for a debriefing which basically consisted of a discussion of how it felt to have shots fired at you.

We tried two more nights, but did little more than cross the river. This time there were shots coming from behind us. We were told that they were support fire, but we could never be certain. The one thing that we learned from these frustrated efforts was that shots being fired are frightening no matter what the source. The one accomplishment was to expose all of us to gunfire which would indeed enable us to react with some confidence when the threat was real. That was the intended outcome.

Our first unit action took place about a week later when, after dark, we formed a long skirmish line and made a simulated attack with a great deal of firing of our weapons. This was to confuse the Germans and make them think the actual attack had begun. We would actually attack from a different location the next morning.

As the sun came up we set out to meet the enemy. Our orders were to move ahead until we encountered opposition. We marched about twenty-five miles before that happened and we took a small group of the enemy prisoner before we found new quarters in another small town. Our division breached the Siegfried Line and began a trip from France, through Germany by crossing the Rhine River, capturing the towns of Mulhausen, Langensalza, Struth and Neumarkt. Next we crossed the Danube River and captured the towns of Regensburg and Passau. Crossing the Danube was the closest we had come to strong resistance. We had to go down a slight hill, rounding a curve which gave us some cover, but then we embarked upon rubber rafts and paddled across the Danube under fire. Upon reaching the other shore, we were in direct fire from machine guns and artillery. We started to dig to get any additional cover from our prone position while our artillery began to pound the Germans. Outgunned, they withdrew and we pursued and caught up to them in Regensburg. It was here that our fist sergeant was wounded and we were trying to get him out of the field of fire. We tried first with our medics, but the Germans fired on them. Then we recruited a couple of German women and put big Red Cross banners on them, but they too were fired upon. The battle continued to rage until we were supported by tanks which opened fire and moved forward to drive the enemy out. We continued to secure the town from any further resistance, but we were unable to save our comrade who became a casualty.

While we were reorganizing after taking the town of Passau there was a rumor that nearby a prisoner of war camp was seeking to surrender. Our platoon sergeant volunteered our platoon to accommodate them. We climbed into the backs of a two and half ton truck and headed for the small town named Giesmar. Since darkness was setting inset in, we were unable to search the entire town, except for the first few houses. We came upon an outpost and took the inhabitants prisoner. They had been on the phone, however, and our presence was known to the Germans.

We continued through town and occupied two connected houses at the other end of the town, where we established a perimeter defense. Because of the small number in our unit, we had to relieve each other every two hours. It was shortly after midnight when we heard shouting and shots. We learned that the guards at the other house had heard prowlers and when challenging them, found them to be a German patrol. Shots were fired, wounding three of the Germans and capturing four others.

One was critically wounded and our Platoon Leader determined that to save his life he would have to be evacuated. He loaded the prisoners and the wounded man on the only truck that remained with us and departed for the return to Passau, taking the company runner and two of our members to guard the prisoners. That depleted our number even further and we now knew that we were in danger of further patrols and greater activity. About dawn we noticed a line of soldiers heading toward us along the road that led into town. At first, white road markers on the edge of the road appeared to be white flags and we thought that we were going to take some prisoners, but as the light became brighter and they got closer we realized that a large number of German soldiers was spreading out in an attack formation.

Our sergeant determined that we were outnumbered and gave the order to retreat. As the first of those in our house headed out the back door and through the yard that led to the roadway, he was fired on by a machine gun that had been set up on a hill and had a pretty clear field of fire into the yard.

My fellow Browning automatic gunner and I were

positioned at the windows that looked out over the roadway. It was our job to keep the attacking force from overrunning our position while the rest made their way out the back door. Each departure was made after a different count. Each person leaving was fired on, but none hit. I was the last to leave and waited for several minutes to hopefully lead the gunner into believing that we had all departed. It must have worked, because I was already behind cover when the burst of machine gun fire began.

As we retraced our steps from the night before and turned into the left fork, we were fired upon again. Our lead scout returned fire and we took the other fork in the road, going to the last house along that route and entered the house to be greeted by a frightened house frau. We told her that we would not harm her and we then set up defensive positions, utilizing every window in the house. Mine was a bay window looking out over an open field and I could see that our two and a half-ton truck had crashed into a tree. Nearby was a jeep with an officer and Walt Offen, a good friend, who was our company runner. They had returned for us with the truck, but were fired on and the truck driver was hit.

We realized that the advancing Germans had proceeded along the road which we had originally used to enter the town and had fired upon the returning truck, causing it to crash and halting the jeep. We could see a line of soldiers approaching the men in the jeep by way of a ditch and calling for them to surrender. Recalling the famous words of General McAuliffe in the Battle of the Bulge, Walt responded with a loud "Nuts!" We were in a good location to be helpful. Every time the Germans stood up to move forward, I could spray them with a burst from my Browning and they took cover.

We then learned that the Officer in the jeep was a forward artillery director who called for artillery fire. One round landed on one side of the ditch, the next on the other and then several rounds landed in the ditch and wiped out the threatening force. We then saw the hillside turn from green to brown as our entire second battalion came toward us in attack formation. They overran any Germans that were left and when we made out location known, we were loaded onto the truck, which was still operative, to head back to Passau. We were not heroes, but we were still alive.

Our final destination was Enns, Austria, where on May 9th we met the 7th Guard Parachute Division of the Russian Army and directed ten armed divisions of German soldiers into an impromptu prisoner of war encampment encircled by a make-shift fence. The Russians had gotten into their line and shot up over two hundred persons, some of whom were civilians who had joined the retreating troops in flight, seeking to surrender to the United States forces rather than to the Russians. Our medics were busy taking care of the wounded.

About a month later I was transferred to the 42nd Infantry Division to prepare for reassignment in the Pacific. I joined them in the town of Salzburg, Austria. Fortunately for me the atomic bomb was dropped and Japan surrendered, so I remained for several months in the army of occupation, spending a good bit of my time in a small village called Kaprun, Austria, nestled in a valley of the Tyrolian Alps. One of my first special assignments was to string a telephone line for the Company Commander from the top of one of the mountains down into the village. This was accomplished by descending in an open gondola hanging from a ski-lift and pulling the wire from a spool located with me in the gondola and allowing it to fall down to the terrain below. It was a hairy experience to say the least, but the phone was put into operation.

On another occasion a buddy of mine and I decided to go up into the mountains and hunt. I carried a carbine because it was light in weight and easily handled. We had not gotten too far up the trail when a bird flew up and I raised the carbine and fired. I missed the bird but suddenly realized that I had no idea where my buddy was when I fired. I could easily have hit him. I unloaded my carbine, returned to the village and have never again gone hunting.

My next move was to attend the Rainbow University located on the edge of a small lake in the village of Zell am Zee where I enjoyed skiing in the Austrian Alps when not in class studying typing, shorthand and Military Administration. We used German Ski trooper equipment and had an Austrian instructor, appropriately named Hans, who had been an instructor in Colorado before the war and had returned to Austria to move his family to the United States, but was drafted into the German Army before he was able to get out. He spoke excellent English.

I was doing very well in my classes until I learned that the General in Vienna was looking for a secretary. From then on I purposely slowed up on my typing and drew pictures for my shorthand. I still managed to pass, but down at a safer level. The 42nd Infantry had been General Mark Clark's outfit and he had imposed a light colored blue scarf that became a part of the uniform and replaced the regulation salute with what was known as the rainbow salute (since the 42nd was called "The Rainbow Division"). I wanted no part of the atmosphere at the division headquarters.

Finally I had enough points to head home. I was sent to Bremerhaven, Germany, to board a ship for America. The trip back was wonderful. We could lounge about on deck and enjoy the early summer weather. It was great to see the Statue of Liberty as we entered the New York Harbor. After a couple of weeks back at Camp Kilmer, NJ, where we were physically evaluated and the dentist filled several teeth with no pain killer, I was met at the gate by my Stepfather and we made the short drive back to Franklinville.

CHAPTER 3

BACK IN CIVIES

Having grown up in Upper Darby, just outside of 69th Street, which was the transportation center for the area and a large shopping site, arriving in Franklinville was something of a letdown. In addition to my folks' store, there was an American store across the street, a skating rink, a firehouse and a gas station strung out along the Delsea Drive. The tiny village was a small break in the otherwise tortuous journey to Cape May, the southern-most area of New Jersey's coastline.

I turned to the gas station owner to find out if there was any excitement in town that I hadn't become aware of and while we were sitting in the station, a Cadillac pulled up parallel to the highway. The driver, a woman, made a beeline for the two-seater outhouse (which served as a rest stop in those days). "Watch this," he said disappearing into the back room. In a moment the door flew open on the outhouse, the woman ran to her car and drove off leaving a cloud of dust. Chuckling, the owner returned. "What just happened?" I asked.

"I have a microphone in the back room," he replied, "and the speaker is the outhouse. I just said 'would you mind moving over one, lady, I'm painting down here?'" (Not a real event-just a joke)

The firehouse had a baseball team. I tried out for the team and became their number one pitcher.

On one occasion, we had a double header scheduled and I pitched the first game, expecting our other pitcher to handle the second, but he came up with a sore shoulder and I wound up pitching both games. A few miles up the highway was the town of Clayton. They not only had a baseball team, but they had a beautiful stadium with lights. I pitched the only game under the lights that I was ever engaged in. Apart from almost getting into a fistfight with their pitcher, all went well and we won the game.

It was the spring of 1946 and I tried to apply for re-entrance into Carnegie Tech but there were so many returning vets wanting to get into college that I was turned down. I then turned to Ursinus College hoping that my scholarship might give me an edge. Although Ursinus could not hold the scholarship for me, they did allow my entrance under the G-I bill and I reported in August for football camp. My parents had prevented me from playing in high school, but I didn't need their permission to play in college so I was free to play.

I made the team and was thrilled to be receiving the opening kick-off against Drexel University in our opening game and to earn four successive letters as a varsity player before graduating in 1950 (Captain in my senior year). I was also privileged to play four years of baseball with a rather successful season in my senior year with five wins and only two losses as a pitcher and playing in the outfield when not pitching, with an overall batting average of 333.

I had won the number one spot during our spring baseball trip. In the last game were playing the Marines at Quantico. They were killing our pitcher and I overheard our athletic manager saying, "Don't worry, they're not our baseballs." I was put in the game and stopped the scoring.

Ursinus offered many extra-curricular activities and I took advantage of several of them, including writing for the weekly newspaper, co-editor of our yearbook, participation in drama productions and several clubs. The faculty was most helpful and I enjoyed my studies immensely. It is fitting to mention that girls and boys were housed in separate facilities and female students were due in their dorm at an early hour.

I graduated Cum Laude with a BA Degree in Business and recognition in Who's Who In American Colleges and Universities, but my most outstanding accomplishment was winning the hand of Mary Elizabeth Ewen in marriage, which took place on June 7, 1950, less than a week after my graduation. She had graduated the year before. I am convinced that it was God's direction that caused me to wind up at Ursinus in order to meet my future wife.

Mary was from Vincentown, a small town in New Jersey where she lived with her parents, Bill and Martha Ewen, two older brothers (Bill and Dave) and a younger sister (Nancy). She was a charming, beautiful young lady with a winning smile and a wonderful disposition. Just to be in her presence was to experience a sense of tranquility.

We were married in a beautiful ceremony in the Vincentown Methodist Church, her church from childhood. It was a candlelight service starting at seven o'clock. At my request the soloist sang "Because." Following a reception in the church basement we were driven by Don and Priscilla Stauffer to New York City for our honeymoon. Pris was a bridesmaid and had been Mary's roommate at Ursinus. She was a native of Manhattan and was going home for a visit.

They dropped us off at the Statler Hotel where we had a reservation. We made the most of our three days in the Big

Apple. We attended a morning television production of Don McNeill's Breakfast Club, attended a Broadway Show, went to the Radio City Music Hall to see the "Rockettes" dance along with a showing of the movie "Father of the Bride" starring Spencer Tracy and a very young Elizabeth Taylor and then we capped it off by attending a baseball game at Yankee Stadium.

The total hotel cost was $29.60, the Broadway show at the Plymouth Theater was $2.00 a ticket, the TV show was without charge and the Yankee's game cost each of us only $1.25, but we weren't sitting behind home plate. We caught a train home to 30th Street Station in Philadelphia. I was to usher in my roommate's wedding in Cheltenham that evening. My brother-in-law, Bill, had driven our 1936 Chrysler to the station and left the keys under the floor mat. I soon found that the car had a flat tire and when I opened the trunk, that tire was flat also. I had to buy two new tubes, but we were still able to make the wedding.

That night we stayed with my folks in Franklinville and went deep sea fishing the next morning with the family. From our marriage on, we had become "George and Mary" in everything we did. We remained married for sixty-two and a half years before she succumbed to a form of dementia in the fall of 2012 and went to be with the Lord. Our life together was a very gratifying and happy one. I do not remember Mary ever being unpleasant or angry. She was always very supportive of me and very productive in her own activities which included work with the YWCA in Pottstown where we first settled, membership in a couple of PTAs, service as a Cub Scout Den Mother and an active member of the Methodist Women.

Later she started selling Avon products and won awards year after year for her efforts. She also served as A Republican Committee Woman in Ambler for several decades, assisting me in my 33 years of community service as a Borough Councilman for eight years, eleven years as Mayor of Ambler and fourteen years as a member of the Pennsylvania House of Representatives.

CHAPTER 4

MARY AND I SET UP HOUSEKEEPING

Our first home was a new apartment in the north end of the town of Pottstown, PA where I had accepted a position as Assistant Manager of Levengood Dairies (established in 1896), at a starting salary of $50 a week. My brother, Bob, had a friend who was relocating to California and wanted to unload his furniture, rather than pay to have it transported to the west coast. We were happy to get it at a bargain price and using a rental truck we moved into Pottstown. The apartment was beautiful and our newly acquired furniture was adequate to meet our needs. The floors were of the sparkling new hardwood variety and we didn't worry about rugs because we enjoyed the wooden surface so much.

Before we had been married we came upon a friendly puppy and Mary's mother agreed to keep it until we had our own place. It was not a large dog and definitely a mixture of something or other, but we loved it. About a year or so later Mary and I went on vacation at the shore with Mary's parents and left the dog with a farmer. When we returned we learned that the dog had tried to escape and broke its leg in the process, so it was sporting a wooden splint. I always played with the dog in the bedroom, rolling from one side of the bed to the other, and calling to the dog who then ran from one side to the other. A few days later, Mary was visiting the woman in the apartment below us who wanted to know why we kept moving the furniture. I covered the bottom of the splint with heavy cloth and stopped playing with the dog.

Levengood Dairies was a home delivery service of milk and dairy products and the manufacturer of ice cream products located in Pottstown with a branch in Norristown. Although I knew nothing of the dairy business, I had majored in business administration and felt that I could be helpful in the running of any business. I did, however, go to Penn State University for short courses in making ice cream and dairy products as well as attending a specialized course in Washington, D.C. featuring the merchandising of dairy products, such as ice cream sundaes, yogurt and other items in order to increase my contribution to the business.

The company was beyond the horse and wagon stage, but the home delivery of milk in glass bottles on a daily basis was a major contribution to the daily routine of most households in the fifties, although it is no longer something that one is likely to encounter. We were in constant competition with super markets and their plastic containers. We went from daily delivery to just delivering three days a week to remain financially sound, which meant that each route salesman had to know two different routes. This became a problem for me, because one of the things that became necessary for me to do when we were short of help, was to relieve some of the salesmen for their vacations. That meant that I was a milk man for that week. This entailed riding with the regular route man at least one day on each route and making notes on where the milk was to be left, along with any other special orders for each customer. It also included noting where angry dogs were located and occasionally information about nipping geese that ran loose. The time of delivery was about five in the morning and it was a lonely existence.

In times of stormy weather and heavy snow, we always doubled up on the trucks so that there would be two men on each truck. I can remember one bad storm when we couldn't get into a village and had to carry the cases of milk, one case in one hand and another between us, across a field of deep snow. The milk was popping up in the bottles as it froze.

It was while at Levengood Dairies that Mary and I moved from Pottstown to Boyertown RD 2, to a thirteen acre farm on top of Rattlesnake Hill. Our daughter, Nancy, had been born in the Pottstown Hospital on May 28, of 1952 and was still a baby. The allure of an old stone farmhouse with a big red barn and several chicken coops was irresistible. The prospect of acquiring a horse (although definitely a swayback), added a potential bonus but we didn't meet the seller's price so he didn't include the horse in the final sale.

That wasn't how my mother-in-law saw the facility, however. Admittedly, it did have some drawbacks. For instance, although it had electricity, the heat was provided by a coal furnace in the basement under an open grate. There were no radiators, only the circulation of hot air which made it to the second floor. The bedrooms were heated by way of open grates in the ceiling of the downstairs rooms.

Water was available from a pump conveniently located on a concrete slab just outside the kitchen. The necessary room was located about fifty feet beyond the front door alongside of one of the chicken coops. It was a deluxe two-seater and except for the bees in the summer, rather comfortable, although no one remained there very long.

Mary and I put together a five year plan. We wanted

to raise collies and we called our new dreamland, "Camelot Kennels." Our stud was a huge collie named Prince Valliant. Teaka was our female and she too was a gorgeous animal. Both were AKC registered. Unfortunately, although the dogs did their job, I was not good at marketing and our kennel plans were frustrated by a lack of sales.

The property was approached from a winding road nearby, from which our tree- lined cobblestone lane wound its way into an opening between the barn and a row of chicken coups, ending rather abruptly at a hedge beyond which there was a large lawn and the residence. The area surrounding the barn was surrounded by green lawn which extended also to the chicken coops. In fact, there was quite a bit of grass which caused some problems in maintenance.

A break in the hedge led to a walkway by which one accessed the house. Immediately inside, an enclosed porch branched off to the left which contained a trap door providing steps to the basement. The furnace was located on a dirt floor. Coal for the furnace was kept in a stall in one of the outbuildings and had to be carried in by a bucket.

Another relic, ashes, had to be carried outside by the same bucket used to bring in the coal. For that matter, coal itself is not a household word in today's jargon, except in reference to providing energy for electric plants or other industrial sites. In those days most homes used coal for heat. They usually had a window in the basement through which the coal was directed to a storage bin by way of a chute. The coal truck backed up, connected the chute, and "shazaam!" the bin was filled in a matter of minutes. Our coal bin was outside and while the stall was quickly filled, it was a different matter getting it to the furnace.

To the right, upon entering the house, was the kitchen. It boasted an electric stove and a refrigerator, but not much else.

There was a table and a couple of chairs, but the absence of a sink and running water immediately caught one's attention. There was no door or wall along the hallway because the entrance continued directly into the dining room which was quite large. There was ample room for a large table and chairs, but to the right of the entrance was a short walkway leading to a set of winding stairs which circled around and above a large, open fireplace. It had been modified from an even larger walk-in fireplace that had graced the room in its former days.

On the floor between the dining room and the large living room to the left was an open grate which measured four feet square. This was directly above the furnace and allowed the hot air to rise and heat the house. It did a pretty good job, but it wasn't a good idea to walk on it, especially in bare feet.

Climbing the circling staircase one found immediately on the right a concrete structure that worked out well as a surface space for storing things such as blankets or clothes. The area above the dining room itself made a very comfortable bedroom. A wall with a door opened into a second bedroom. The floors in both rooms had grates about a foot in diameter to allow hot air to rise and heat the rooms.

The walls of the house were stone and were about three feet thick. They kept the cold out as long as there was a fire in the furnace. I guess the thick walls and the open fireplace had a lot to do with the overall concept of how interesting the house was, although the big red barn, the grounds surrounding it and their potential also played a role in creating the environment which attracted Mary and me.

Living in this romantic environment proved to have many challenges but Mary was a trooper and we enjoyed our existence there, although we never made it through our five years. Needless to say, we made a few changes. The first was to put in running water and get a sink in the kitchen and a tub and sink in the house. Since there was no place to put the bathroom except for the enclosed porch, that's where it wound up. We installed an electric pump and the piping necessary to provide water to the kitchen and bathroom. One continuing problem was that the water was still cold and we never actually corrected that, relying instead on the stove to heat water.

Another major problem presented itself, however. Since the porch contained the only access to the basement, it now became necessary to create a new entrance. To do that I attacked the outside wall below the porch area, dug through the dirt and then broke through the foundation so that I could install a doorway. It made a convenient way in with the coal bucket but since it was around the side of the house with a fairly high hedge running from the side of the house, out, and across the front yard, Mary was not at all inclined to make that trip during the day and definitely not going to chance it after dark. Consequently, she never had the pleasure of walking on the dirt floor of the basement. Since the furnace needed to be kept filled with coal, if I had a meeting at night, it usually required my making a new fire and banking it when I got home, before I could go to bed. It didn't take long to get an oil burner installed.

There was so much green grass in the yard that it took six hours to cut it. Because I was working six days a week, that pretty much tied up my Sundays. Using a push-type mower it was tough work, especially in the heat of summer. I noticed a used new-fangled aluminum power mower for sale. I had heard that gasoline powered mowers were pretty special so I bought "the answer to my prayers" and took it home. It now took me three hours to start the motor and three hours to cut the lawn. All that glitters isn't gold.

The first gasoline powered mower was made in 1919 by Colonel Edwin George. It was not used very much until after

WWII, but by the early 60s they had come into extensive use. Improvements, including the substitution of electricity for gasoline, have continued to make the task easier and quieter.

Another questionable asset of our challenging enterprise was an antique Farmall tractor with metal wheels that were six feet in diameter. It was used to cut the growth that continued to occupy the section of field that bordered the street, using a cutter-blade connected by means of a two-by-four piece of lumber. The wheels had metal spikes that were about four inches in length and they caused the tractor (and its driver) to rock back and forth as it made its way over the hard surface of the road to get to the field. To further complicate matters, the field contained several hidden rocks which repeatedly broke the tow bar and necessitated cutting a new one and replacing it.

In less than a year, Mary was expecting our second child. Richard was born in the Pottstown Hospital on November 2, of 1953 and when it came time to bring him home, there was a heavy coating of snow on the highway. I was concerned about climbing the hill in my automobile, so I borrowed the pickup truck from work. We made it with no difficulty, but that kind of filled our living quarters. When we discovered two years later that our third child was expected, we thought that we should not mention it to Mary's mother until we could precede that announcement with word of a larger house and many additional facilities.

We found just what we wanted, back in Pottstown at 128 Chestnut Street. It was a three story house with two and a half baths and situated on a postage stamp for a lawn that I could cut with a pair of scissors. Five bedrooms, oil heat with radiators and no outside work, except for a small garden in the rear. What a find, but now we had to find a buyer for our special domain.

We advertised and finally a heavy set man came to look at it. The floor shook as he walked through from the dining room to the living room and dishes rattled on the shelves of the china closet. He made a remark about housing his in-laws in the outbuildings, but we were only interested in getting his down payment and signature on the bill of sale. Having accomplished that, we made settlement on the house in town and looked forward to a life of ease and contentment. Our third child, George William was born on July 31, of 1956 in the Pottstown Hospital. We didn't think he would like being called Junior, so we started just calling him George William although some tried to make "Buddy" stick. He is also affectionately called "King" George because of an association he got into at the Holiday Inn. He answers to any one of them, but most just call him George.

We Move Back Into Town

One evening Mary was watching the news on television when she let out a cry and called me to come quickly. When I arrived I was shocked to see a chimpanzee rolling across our former living room floor on roller skates. We found out that the new tenant had a number of the hairy protégés with which he toured to feature in special shows. These were the "in-laws" to which he had made reference when he was looking over our house earlier. I determined to never go back to the area for fear of what our neighbors might have felt about our selling to him, but we never had a clue before this revelation on our black and white television set.

We received a major setback shortly after returning to Pottstown. A blacksmith shop was located just above us on Chestnut Street. He stopped me one day and asked what was causing my daughter, Nancy, to limp. He had noticed it as she walked past his shop on the way to school. Neither Mary nor I had noticed a limp, but when we questioned her, she admitted to having some difficulty in walking and we immediately made arrangements to have it examined by our family doctor. The results were that she had a condition known as "Perthes" disease which is a softness in the bone structure in the hip area and the treatment is to refrain from putting any weight on that area. This would be accomplished by using crutches and keeping that leg in a sling. Nancy was not happy but quickly mastered the use of crutches. She was even less happy about the carping of other children who accused her of faking the injury, because there was no outward sign of the problem.

In the meantime I had evaluated my position with the dairy and decided that a career change was in order. I applied for a sales job, and was hired by the Sun Life Insurance Company of Canada. Selling life insurance was certainly different but I was convinced that I was really helping people prepare for later life. I felt good for having made a sale. Naturally my family was number one in my prospect list and I managed to cover most of my family and my in-laws. Then it got a lot tougher and although I continued to make sales, the numbers were not producing the kind of money needed to meet expenses, so I applied for a substitute teaching job and became listed in the Pottstown Schools as well as the Pottsgrove School District to supplement my income.

I should mention that my personal life insurance purchases were the most important financial decisions that I have ever made. When we had a chance to purchase a beautiful home across the street from our location on Mattison Avenue in Ambler, it was made possible through borrowing on my insurance. Subsequently, Sun Life went public and all policy holders were given stock in the company which continues to this day to pay helpful dividends.

I had majored in Math in College and so that was what I was called for mostly, but I also found that the schools liked my size for handling shop classes. I was particularly unpopular in study halls where it was my mistaken idea that students would have work to do. One student asked me on my first arrival if we would play Peter Gunn as they did with the other teacher. I took a piece of paper and wrote out a long division problem for him and told him to sit down and get to work. I was never able to sit down throughout the study hall, because I had to constantly walk around, checking to see if the students were working. If not, they also received special math problems.

In Math, I was asked on one occasion to serve for a long period of several months in one class and I was horrified to find that the students were not prepared for seventh grade Math. We spent a lot of time reviewing the basics. It was really disappointing because I saw Math as a way of life. The same process used in solving a problem in Math could be applied to the problems in life and these students were missing that opportunity.

I was approached by Tom Sellers, who had supplied Levengood Dairies with their chocolate flavoring for chocolate milk and the cocoa powder for their chocolate ice cream. We had become good friends and Tom asked me if I would like to come to Ambler and run his business for him. The company that had been processing his product was going to operate only a few days and he could not get along with that kind of a supply system, so he was going to build a new plant in Ambler and wanted someone to help out.

His product was excellent. I had pushed our route salesmen to use it when soliciting new customers. Milk is milk and it was hard to show why our milk was better than another dairy's milk, but one taste of our chocolate milk and the sale was made. God was opening another door and we moved to 351 Mattison Avenue in Ambler. It was a beautiful three story stone house on a wide street with lots of shade that did not get a lot of traffic.

CHAPTER 5

AMBLER, OUR NEW NEIGHBORHOOD

I was so impressed with the neighborhood that I suggested that Mary not leave the clothes line up after taking down the wash. She agreed. We didn't want to offend our new neighbors. We moved in during the summer and on the occasion of my first outdoor activity, I was mowing the lawn. Since we had come from such a small yard in Pottstown, I had junked the power mower and now purchased another push-type mower because, while the new yard was larger, it was not a six hour operation. The temperature was way up there and I was soaking wet from perspiration when suddenly our next door neighbor, Cliff Downing, approached me with a bottle of beer and offered it to me. While I was not a drinker, I couldn't refuse such generosity and nothing ever tasted so good. Cliff and I became best friends as did my wife, Mary, and Josephine, Cliff's wife.

My desire to make a good impression on the neighborhood failed however, when, after having had a good day's fishing at the shore, I cleaned the fish and left the trimmings in a box in the garage to be put out for the trash man. Unfortunately I forgot to put them out and one day when I came home from work Mary greeted me with the news that something out back smelled bad. I remembered the fish and buried the remains.

We were unable to take any of our dogs with us to Ambler and Nancy missed her dogs terribly. A puppy was the one thing that she wanted for Christmas. I searched the newspapers for a puppy and checked the SPCA to no avail. I was looking for a collie. Time was running out and I was finally able to find a six month old puppy listed in the weekly paper, but it was not a collie. I called the owner and she described the pup as a wonderful Golden Retriever whose disposition with children was impeccable. She finally stated with great pride that he could sit on the ice for hours and not even shiver because of a special layer of fat beneath the skin that kept him comfortable in spite of a dip in the thermometer. How could I resist?

I drove the short distance to where the dog was located and was surprised at his size. At six months he was huge, but his great friendliness was convincing. His tail never stopped wagging. We returned home. It was late afternoon on Christmas Eve but luckily the children had not returned from play and I was able to get him into our basement. We sent the children to bed early so that we could decorate the tree and assemble some presents. Not a whimper was heard from our new family member in the basement.

Christmas morning arrived and the children woke us early with the usual anxiety and excitement. It has been our tradition to allow the children to remove the contents of their stockings hung from the mantle, next we would have breakfast and then open presents. In spite of all the activity there was not a sound from below. After all of everyone's presents had been opened, Nancy was obviously disappointed that she had not gotten her puppy.

I asked her to get a bag for the trash from the top of the cellar stairs and we all watched as she opened the door and unleashed seventy some pounds of reddish brown fur which jumped on her, knocking her to the floor and the two wrestled for several moments as Rusty, our first of several Golden Retrievers became an official member of our family.

Mary embarked upon a long term campaign of selling Avon products. She won many annual awards for her efforts, and endeared herself to her customers. In another area, our two oldest sons, Rich and George William, got into the business of delivering the morning Inquirer. I admired their enthusiasm and initiative until the weekend, when they awoke me and wanted me to go with them. What I found was a pile of newspapers that climbed about six feet into the morning air. The Sunday paper was thick and the pile awaiting them was clearly more than I would be comfortable leaving for them to deliver. We entered into a family partnership and I took them around in our station wagon each week thereafter. We also embarked upon a quality control program wherein I insisted that they put the papers inside the screen door if it opened and if not, to be sure that it would be out of bad weather. It was a service that was greatly appreciated by their customers.

My first assignment in my new job was to travel to New Jersey where the dairy powder processing plant was located in order to learn the process. Next I was to supervise the building of a plant that would house the mixing equipment, have easy access to trucks bringing in raw products and provide easy shipping as well. Tom had chosen an excellent site on North Main Street and in no time at all we were in business. Tom Sellers was a genius. He not only had a tremendous mind for finance, but was also able to formulate a special formula for making chocolate milk.

Chocolate milk in those days had to be shaken before drinking because the chocolate would settle out. Tom was aware that chocolate does not dissolve in milk which results in the chocolate sinking to the bottom of the container. He also discovered that a stabilizer would form shelves which kept the chocolate particles suspended in the bottle and eliminated the settlement problem. Most suppliers of chocolate flavoring to dairies delivered it in liquid form using tank trucks. The dairies then had to use valuable storage tanks to keep the chocolate until they were ready to mix their chocolate milk.

These two items added cost to the flavoring, but it was the use of a stabilizer that really gave us the advantage and it paid off in increased business. Tom was able to mix all the necessary ingredients in powder form and package it in bags according to the size of the batch the dairies wanted to mix. This freed their storage vats and reduced the cost of delivering considerably. Tom's formula became popular and he was the supplier of choice of many dairies in and around the area. No one knew it was Sellers' chocolate, however, because the finished product carried the dairy's name, not his.

My work was very satisfying as well as challenging. It required lifting fifty pound bags of cocoa and hundred pound bags of sugar, so I didn't have to join the YMCA to get exercise. But in addition, I did a lot of lab work to develop new formulas for making Vanilla Fudge ice cream and a new formula for making bottled ice tea. It also called for sales work on days when not in production and I really enjoyed selling the many advantages of our product to prospective dairies. I especially enjoyed the variety of assignments which my employment made available.

My next door neighbor was an expert at getting me involved with the community. It all began when I was complaining that the adults were using the children to earn money to finance the adult softball program. I had gotten involved with coaching one of the children's little league baseball teams and it bothered me that money raised for that purpose was being diverted into the adult program. Cliff, who was on the local Recreation Committee enabled me to join him there and the matter was soon straightened out.

CHAPTER 6

DUTY CALLS

I also became involved in matters of the Borough Council and was able to get appointed from Ambler's Third Ward. I found the work both interesting and challenging so at the completion of the unexpired time of my term, I ran my first political campaign to get officially elected to that position. I canvassed the ward, stopping at every house to introduce myself and talk to the constituents. I was successful in the election, but my success was largely due to my wife's contacts through church and Avon and my children through their school contacts and the paper route.

Not long after I began serving as a councilman It occurred to me that the Mayor was not utilizing the full potential of his office. Since he was of the opposite party, I decided to challenge him and extended my visits to the entire borough, making my case that the mayor could be far more productive and pledging to make it happen. Once again I was successful and became the "chocolate Mayor".

The chief responsibility of the Mayor is the police department. Since I knew nothing of police work I enrolled in a course in Police Administration at the Montgomery

County Community College which was located at that time in Conshohocken. We were plagued with a drug problem and while it was not confined to the borough, it was definitely something that needed attention. I included Drug Abuse and Juvenile Delinquency in my curriculum and was able to utilize much of what I learned in all three areas.

One thing that stood out in my mind from my Police Administration studies was that crime occurs in the absence of the police. At the time we operated a police car with two occupants which followed a regular schedule. I insisted that we use two cars and vary the schedule to increase the presence of the police throughout the borough which would make it more difficult for anyone to know just where or when the patrol car would arrive.

One thing that would be required however was the purchase of radios so that there would be dependable communication with the cars and the station. Our communications system was not very satisfactory, but the President of Council did not want to put out the money to correct the situation. I suggested that my Advisory Committee would hold a special, well-advertised, fund-raising bake sale to come up with the money and he capitulated.

The drug problem was not as easy to correct. I did learn that drugs were thought to fill some kind of need and that one way to deal with the problem was to introduce some new form of activity. I decided to form a youth program and we were able to rent the Ambler Theater which at the time lay vacant. I suggested the name "AHOY," standing for Ambler Help Our Youth. The young people however, turned that down saying that they didn't need help, they needed an opportunity and I challenged them to come up with their own name. They chose "Rising Sun" standing for the rise of a new day. While "Rising Sun" still had connotations in my mind to the war with the

Japanese in the Pacific, I yielded to their wishes and we became known as Rising Sun.

The young people operated the theater, sold tickets, ushered and selected the movies. We had to hire a union projectionist and the committee selected a John Wayne movie, True Grit, for the opening night. The film broke at least three times and we endured clapping sessions, but somehow those difficulties were overcome and the movies became better quality. The William Penn Foundation was a real life saver in terms of funding and the Rotary Club of Ambler repaired the stage. The Ambler Theater in its hay day had been an outstanding vaudeville theater. We hosted several on-stage productions including "Jesus Christ, Superstar", Hall and Oates in their formative days and a totally local production under the direction of the Kearse Dance Studios with an International Holiday theme called "Festivals".

Olin Kearse made costumes with many imported materials and we invited Ambassadors from several countries who were stationed in Philadelphia. We entertained them for dinner and delivered them to a red carpet reception at the theater entrance complete with three trumpeters. They were ushered to their seats with the playing of their national anthems. The participants in the show were all local people.

At that time the borough was not decorated for Christmas and we enlisted volunteers from the Jaycees who decorated large sheets of plywood with fresh cut greens and twinkle lights which were suspended from telephone poles up and down Butler Avenue. We hired a special lift truck to make the installation. It was a classic community event in which the young people starred.

The drug problem persevered. I decided to take one of our policemen out of uniform and have him operate as a detective, focusing mainly on the drug problems. We cooperated with the county detectives and employed a drug abuse specialist to head up a program designed to focus on other ways to deal with the problem. We also cooperated closely with the school system. While we didn't totally resolve the situation we made a serious dent in the operation.

We initiated special recognition of merchants throughout the borough by presenting a "Merchant of the Month" award to help them with their competition problems with the malls which were becoming a serious challenge. Parking was always cited as a major problem even though you could walk downtown from your home easier than parking at some of the more distant parking spots in the mall parking lots. And parking meters were cited as deterrents but without them store employees would likely park there and occupy the space all day long so that there would be no place for customers to park.

Mary and I celebrated the birth of our fourth child, a son, whom we named Robert, after my brother. Shortly thereafter we faced a serious challenge when our nine year old son, George, was rendered unconscious in the Borough Park on Friday 13, 1965. I was summoned from work and found him being loaded into the Ambler Community Ambulance. Our family doctor, Dr. Kelton was taking care of him and suggested that I get Mary and meet them at the Chestnut Hill Hospital. We had to get someone to take care of our newborn son, Robert, who had been born about three and a half months earlier on May 31.

We were met at the hospital by Dr. Padula (an Ursinus graduate) who was the brain specialist in charge. He told us that while they had some ideas about his injuries, they could not really diagnose them fully. George had evidently been injured somewhere near the back of his ear and they were checking for pressure. We would just have to wait it out. The supposition, since he was found alone, was that he had somehow fallen from a tree and struck a rock. He had been playing with a neighbor earlier. We subsequently learned that he had been struck by a rock. Our good friend Josephine Downing organized a twenty-four hour prayer vigil at Calvary Church and throughout the long duration of the crisis, church members were wonderful, helping take care of young Rob and providing food and consolation.

Wait and worry we did. George remained unconscious for a period of five weeks. Mary and I took shifts sitting with him, reading and playing music because we were told that in similar cases, the person, though unconscious was often aware of what was going on. Early in the process I had prayed for some sign and that night dreamed that he opened his eyes and smiled. I was certain that things would work out, but the situation continued to be contentious. George was kept on a bed of ice to keep the flow of blood to his brain to a minimum, reducing the potential permanent brain damage that he might suffer.

Strangers stopped and offered to pray for him as did a Catholic priest. We welcomed all prayers and our minister, Paul Beck, was most helpful. The staff at the hospital was very supportive, but the prognosis did not seem to improve. Mary held him on her lap and sang and read to him. George became well known on the other floors. Then, after five weeks, one day Mary was holding him and he began to smile and then laugh. Mary felt a warm stream of moisture which was the cause of his mirth. He had wet on her. All she could do was cry with relief and joy.

I hastened to join them and his recovery from that point on was remarkable, but not without the help of a young nurse who took a special interest in him. She had him up and pushing a chair down the hall to get him walking. He had to relearn everything. Speech was difficult. He made a hit with everyone when he asked a riddle which was very interrupted as he found difficulty in getting it out. The riddle was, "What do you get when you cross a lemon and a cat?" The answer, which he revealed with a grin, "A sour puss." He was challenged by the speech therapist to say "Methodist Episcopal" which was the ultimate test. He was given the weekend to achieve it and by Monday he was able to respond in a very slow and determined fashion, "Me-tho-dist E-pis-co-pal." Eating was also a difficult task which had to be overcome. The plan was to teach us how to feed him through a tube, but our young nurse friend introduced him to a taffy and he began to suck on it which led to his ability to swallow and eat regularly. Again, a church friend, Marion Sutter, tutored him and he attended a special school in Norristown for a year, but was able to return to his regular class and did not lose any time. He later went out for the junior high school football team but Dr. Kelton was the team physician and put an end to that endeavor. His recovery was complete.

CHAPTER 7

THE HARRISBURG CHALLENGE

Conditions in Harrisburg were such that I saw them as being bad for our borough as well as our business. It seemed that something needed to be done and I determined to seek office as a State Representative. Running for state office is far more complex than just running for local office. I soon found that to be the case as I attempted to run a campaign for the office of state representative in the 151st Legislative District. Using those workers who had previously supported me, I set forth to prepare literature and, realizing that there were 32 voting polls that I needed to have workers, I began to recruit additional help.

I was running against an incumbent who had been in office for eight years. My personal evaluation of his performance was such that I felt justified in seeking his removal. However the process is more complex as I soon learned. Although I felt that I had campaigned well and that my literature was self- descriptive, in the primary election I was defeated. In evaluating the reasons and in discussion with other party members I came to realize that a great deal of preparatory work would be necessary in order to accomplish my goal. I began that work in earnest.

It included the realization that the election process was far more involved than simply getting one's name on the ballot. There were a lot of people in each of the districts that needed to be contacted and convinced that what I was offering would be beneficial to the electorate which they represented. There was also an obvious necessity to reach out to the party organization at the county level and I began that effort as well. I also learned that the incumbent required another term in office in order to qualify for continued health benefits. This was not only important to him but a factor that would be considered by many whose assistance I would need.

For that reason I began to plan, not for the next election, but the one following. However I began immediately to make the acquaintances necessary, the contacts that were necessary and to put together a more comprehensive election organization. In that regard I was assisted by many persons who included Evan Michener, who would become my campaign manager, and Lou Guerra, who became my financial manager. Lou was well-established in the party and very influential in helping me make contact with needed supporters.

When the right time came we contacted the party chairman and requested a conference which would direct party support for the winning candidate. That conference was granted and I was able to become the endorsed candidate of our party. We engaged in extensive door-to-door canvassing, a substantial mass mailing effort and took advantage of every opportunity to appear publicly. This time I emerged victorious and was elected the representative of the 151st Legislative District in the Pennsylvania House of Representatives.

The regular schedule for the house was three days a week. The occasion of my swearing-in in Harrisburg in

January was a most memorable event shared with my wife and many family members. The physical structure of the capitol building is one of the most outstanding architectural accomplishments throughout the United States. I have indeed had the opportunity to visit many of the capitols throughout the country and concluded that there is none finer than that of the Commonwealth of Pennsylvania.

The big joke for freshmen legislators was that the first order of business was to find the location of the restrooms. I truly believe that the most important contributor to my legislative experience was my secretary, Theresa Rosivack Boyer. I had no part in selecting her, but had I had the opportunity, I could not have made a better choice. Her knowledge of the process was fundamental to my being able to address the responsibilities that went with the position. She handled phone calls, directed me to staff members of the various committees that were necessary in studying proposed legislation and answered all of my many questions.

There is no doubt in my mind that the most fortunate opportunity came my way when I was contacted by a woman named Marie Tursi. She was a resident of Horsham, a part of my district, who described to me very succinctly what had happened as a result of a drunk driver crashing into the automobile being driven by her son on the way to his high school prom. He was killed and his mother was notably distraught. She had determined to take upon herself a campaign to reduce such crashes. Her big request was to form a state-level committee to draft appropriate legislation.

I immediately enlisted our staff person from the transportation committee and asked that appropriate penalties be established to punish drivers who are under the influence of alcohol or drugs. Fortunately, almost at the same time Governor Dick Thornburgh had invited freshmen legislators to join him for breakfast. He was a most congenial host and I had an opportunity to request the formation of a drunk-driving task force. He agreed and assigned the head of the Pennsylvania State Police as well as the head of the Department of Transportation to the Task Force. Legislation was prepared and circulated for additional sponsors. As the prime sponsor it was my responsibility to manage the debate on the House floor. We were supported by favorable press coverage but confronted by a strong effort on the part of the trial lawyers to reduce or at least offer an opening to soften the mandatory sentences which we were included in the legislation. There were many examples of judges imposing sentences selectively. We wanted no exemptions and in the end we succeeded in getting the bill passed without amendment.

The battle in the Senate was another challenge but fortunately their leadership stood firm and once again the bill remained intact. Perhaps my most thrilling experience in Harrisburg was to be seated on one side of Gov. Thornburgh with Marie Tursi on the other while he signed her bill into law.

One of the greatest rewards in my 14 years as a state representative was the opportunity to assist people with problems they encountered. There is no doubt that the right person in the right position can make things happen and we were able to do that for many people in many circumstances.

As a member of the Ambler Kiwanis Club I had a dual opportunity to establish a project for students in the Wissahickon School District known as" There Ought To Be a Law". Over a period of several years in cooperation with wonderful teachers we received many suggestions for which each student was duly recognized. Many of these were researched and in some cases introduced as a potential law. The one which stands out in my memory was offered by a young lady who suggested that the law on reporting missing children as it stood allowed for a couple of days to pass before a missing child was reported to the authorities. She pointed out that in spite of the fact that perhaps the child was simply visiting, the fact of the matter is that the longer the delay in responding, the less likely the police are to find the missing child. We drafted the law mandating immediate reporting and response and it passed. This young lady also sat beside the governor as he signed her suggestion into law.

There were many other pieces of legislation during my 14 years that were significant, but these two had special memories attached. While the house officially met for only three days a week, that period of time was greatly expanded in the adoption of the budget each year. For some reason this process always seems to involve late-night sessions which precede the adjournment for the summer. They included many special meetings, special deals and in many cases a great deal of pressure in the process of hammering out the document which in most cases was really not favored in its totality by anyone.

In addition to regular session days there are many committee meetings and they could take place anywhere in the state. We celebrated the birthday of the US Constitution in Independence Hall in Philadelphia and took a train ride from outside Gettysburg on which a simulated Abe Lincoln also traveled. When the train reached Gettysburg it was met by a contingency of union soldiers on horseback who escorted the president to the famous cemetery to repeat the Gettysburg Address.

One thing that I insisted on doing while in office was writing my own newsletter. Our public relations people were perfectly willing to do so for us in what I consider to be a generic way. I wanted to speak frankly and personally to my constituents about what I was doing and why I was doing it. I learned very quickly how very limited I was in knowledge.

I wanted and needed input from persons who had personal experience if possible and I depended quite heavily on our staff people whose job it was to constantly research and stay on top of issues relating to their specific committee assignments. In every case I was exceedingly pleased with their efforts.

Over the period of the seven terms (14 years) which I served in Harrisburg, I was given the opportunity to serve on many different committees. Each of these was important but some held more significance personally than others. For instance I was most interested in health and welfare matters, matters concerning conservation and the environment, matters of education and especially federal-state relations, on which I served as minority chairman during the last few years I was in Harrisburg.

In that capacity, on several occasions with the aid of our staff person, we arranged to go to Washington D.C. and meet with our party representatives from the Commonwealth of Pennsylvania. These meetings were very productive and were well received. Our number one objective was to describe the damage done by unfunded federal legislation impacting our Commonwealth without concern for the financial burden it placed upon the state legislature.

A very gratifying opportunity presented itself for me to become a member of the American Legislative Exchange Council which consisted of members from state legislatures throughout the nation. While the overall considerations were widespread, I served on the task force on Energy, Environment and Natural Resources. ALEC journeyed to locations throughout the United States to conduct special meetings and take part in conventions which covered a much wider spectrum of subjects.

I served as chairman of the task force for seven years and as such was involved in establishing various presentations involving our subject matter. In that capacity and certainly with the assistance of the staff we were able to attract nationally known speakers. We were also able to propose specific legislative concepts which were included in regularly published journals for distribution in the many states. It was my special honor to have received a bust of Thomas Jefferson and the designation of Outstanding Alec Legislator for the legislative year of 1991 to 1992.

When in 1994 I determined that there were many aspects of state government with which I strongly disagreed, it caused me to decide to run for the office of Lieutenant Governor as a running mate for Tom Ridge, the gubernatorial candidate. I believed that it might be possible as part of the administration to address some of the problems which I felt existed. It really seems almost impossible to function when House members face reelection every two years. This means that having been elected as a legislator and with the new session beginning in January, everything has to start from scratch. At the end of the session just completed, all legislation remaining under consideration is dropped from the schedule. New committees are appointed, in many instances new chairman are put in place and every piece of legislation has to be reintroduced, sent to committee and must proceed through the rules before it can be considered, all of which is extremely time consuming.

Once reorganized, the process of committee meetings, introducing new legislation, assignment of committees, consideration of legislation and then the daily operation of the house which includes attendance, announcements and other business takes preference over the required movement on the calendar that legislation must undergo before a vote is taken. All of this drags out and before long the main attraction is the consideration of the budget which is in and of itself, extremely time consuming.

After the budget is passed, the summer recess follows and then the legislative business resumes in September. This is the critical time for the consideration of legislation, because after the recess for Christmas, attention focuses on the upcoming election process. Herein lies the major difficulty. Consideration of legislation necessitates leadership looking carefully at how any proposed legislation may or may not influence the outcome of the next election.

The big driving factor in the makeup of the legislature is the numbers game. Whichever party has the larger number controls who will be the Speaker of the House, who will then control who will chair all the committees and the makeup of the committees because there is a numerical majority of the majority party in each case. This whole process can best be described as "control." Another major difficulty is the policy of longevity. For the most part committee appointments are made according to the length of service of the members. The Majority Leader controls who will be chairman of each committee and the Minority Leader controls who will be sub-chairman of each committee. It isn't necessary to point out that the road which new legislation must take is not only bumpy, but also subject to many detours.

While I thought that I had some answers to some of these problems, they were not well received by leadership. I thought, however, that they might be considered by the electorate. The following is a quote from my news release: "In announcing his candidacy for Lieutenant Governor, seven term Representative George E. Saurman of Montgomery County characterized himself as a modern day Paul Revere. 'It is not the British who are coming,' said Saurman, "it is the persistent erosion of the very principles which have made America great."

What I didn't face was the reality that, particularly in the case of a running mate for the endorsed candidate for

Governor, the party leaders were not seeking solutions but rather looking for voting support for that candidate. In my case the name Schweiker offered far more state recognition since Dick Schweiker had been a popular United States Senator from Pennsylvnia and even though Lieutenant Governor candidate, Mark Schweiker, was not related to him, the name was still important.

While I could have continued to run as a State Representative, I believed that the honorable thing to do was to declare my intentions and therefore I did not seek reelection to the House. This whole decision was made in consultation with my wife and those who had supported me in my position as State Representative. While I missed my colleagues in Harrisburg and the opportunity to continue serving my loyal constituents, I firmly believe it was the right decision. And so at the end of my term in 1994, I bid farewell to Harrisburg.

A vacancy existed in the slate for local offices in Ambler and I reentered the political ring, running once more for Borough Council. I was elected and during the last two years I served as President of Council. During that time I requested advice from RSVP, an organization of retired executives who volunteer their time to small businesses and in our case to local government. One of the persons who served in that capacity is a man named Bernie Roseman. His advice and counsel particularly regarding the process of purchasing was most helpful. He and I continue to meet on a fairly regular basis to share ideas and Bernie has joined me on the board of Montgomery County Senior Adult Activities Center where he continues to offer excellent insight.

During the time that we lived on Mattison Avenue we were quite content. Mary took special notice of a neighbor who lived on the other side of the street and tried hard to see that she was taken care of. She was a piano teacher and our daughter, Nancy, took lessons from her but also was the deliverer of many special food items that Mary prepared for her teacher.

Another neighbor lived directly across the street from us at 360 Mattison Avenue. The home belonged to Charlie Korn who was a stock broker and harbored two Cadillac's in his two and half car garage. His wife had died and he cared for his sister-in-law. Mildred was a typical New Englander. It was rumored that Charlie had had the large, three-story home constructed on the model of the home his wife and family lived in in New England in order to convince her to join him in Pennsylvania. It was truly a beautiful structure. We used to describe it to our friends when they were visiting--- describe it, tell them to park in front, and then cross the street to our house.

Charles Korn was not a very socially minded individual. He would always say hello when we met on the occasion of carrying out the trash. One day he called and asked if I would come over. He was confined to bed. He didn't want to call a doctor or nurse and I tried to look after him, though I remained in contact with his family doctor. One day he became extremely ill and I called the doctor who came and stayed with him until he passed on. After his death, Mary made trips fairly regularly to check on Mildred. I did minor repairs to the house, such as replacing window panes, etc. Mildred did not survive her brother-in-law by many months.

After her passing we received a phone call from a mutual friend indicating that he was administering the estate and was establishing a silent auction for the property. He wanted to know if we would like to enter a bid, recognizing the relationship that we had with the family. Mary and I talked it over and decided to do so, although we had no idea what to offer. We had our home appraised, took account of all money available from borrowing on our life insurance policies, threw in our cash in the bank and entered our bid. It turned out that we were two hundred dollars above a contractor who wanted to tear down the carriage house and build another house in its place and even build on the lot on the other side of the house. We were not only able to get the house, but also retain the integrity of the neighborhood. God was active once more and we thanked Him.

The house had a huge enclosed side porch that served beautifully for my district office, for which I never charged the state. It had a private entrance from the outside and easily accommodated all of the equipment that made for an efficient, easily accessible office for my constituents.

Mary's mother was living alone after her husband passed on and was beginning to have trouble managing. The family had gotten together and tried to persuade her to move into a retirement facility in New Jersey, but she would have none of it. Mary and I discussed the situation and decided that it would be possible to turn Charlie's two and a half car garage into a lovely cottage with a living room, kitchen and bedroom on the first floor and the entire upstairs for a second bedroom. We talked to her mother about it, stressing that she could move most of her furniture into it and be near Mary. She agreed, we got zoning for a "mother-in-law' house and construction began. She was quite happy for several years but her condition began to worsen and the strain on Mary was becoming more stressful.

Mary's sister, Nancy, had been divorced and her children were all out of the house so she offered to come down and stay on the second floor and help with their mother. Although her mother passed on, Nancy remained in the cottage and we were able to negotiate that she could continue there when the new owners of our house took over. That's where things still stand.

CHAPTER 8

BEHIND THE SCENES

I firmly believe that God was in control of my life. Looking back, there is no explanation for how things progressed without some outside force helping to steer the ship of state. Many people had a part in making the wheels go around, but even so, their presence at the times they appeared and the influence they provided seemed to be directed. There is no doubt that my grandfather influenced me throughout my life. He instilled ideas of responsibility and honesty, but also a reliance on God which was invaluable in combat, in high school and college and throughout my married life and professional opportunities. In school, my homeroom teacher in junior high, Miss Corey; my Latin teacher, Lucile Noble and my English teacher, Helen Feree in high school all influenced me in my progress. Abe Quay, my step-father was a level headed individual who filled the responsibilities that were lacking because of the separation of my mother and father. My oldest brother, Dick, who was only with us for a short period of time, nonetheless provided valuable insight into how to meet challenges and deal with people. My other brother, Bob, filled the role of my "older brother" and did so throughout my life until the day that he pulled off to the side of the road and said, "Oh no" and passed on to eternity. What courage and what strength! Certainly someone to emulate.

My wife, whom I consider to be the most wonderful woman in the world, and my children who have been so loyal and devoted, all coming to the rescue in so many challenges in different ways and at different times. In business, Gordon Astheimer, gave me my first job opportunity, Tom Sellers taught me so much about the business world. In politics Evan Michener, whose support carried me to Harrisburg and Lou Guerra, who provided inside information about political relationships that enabled me to be of service to my community and to the Commonwealth of Pennsylvania. A host of individuals, unrelated in many ways, and yet tied together in the web of progression needed to move me forward in God's plan.

Mixed throughout the years were many opportunities for pleasure. Vacation trips were frequent and productive. We had a twenty foot cabin cruiser on which we spent many days afloat on Barnegat Bay. We spent many days visiting my brother, Bob, in his home on Long Beach Island. He was a dedicated surf fisherman whose greatest joy seemed to be when I would tie into one of the huge fish that used to frequent the waters of the Atlantic Ocean just at the end of 29th Street in Ship bottom. Bob had retired to what had been a summertime cottage. He and his wife, Grayce, had winterized the building and they had given up their residence in Runnymede, New Jersey and moved to the shore. We were always welcome and spent many hours surf fishing on the beach. Bob was not only an avid fisherman but a student of the process and we enjoyed very much the time we spent together.

Mary and I were able to reciprocate by inviting them to join us at many of the wonderful places that our timeshare made possible. This included the Outer Banks of North Carolina, Williamsburg, Virginia, (where are timeshare was located), Cape Cod, Massachusetts and Fredericksburg, Virginia. Bob had assumed the role of big brother and truly kept his eye out for me as I fulfilled my life. No one could ask for a better counselor, friend or fishing instructor.

Neither Mary nor I had any serious health problems but the big house in Ambler was becoming something of a burden, rather than a place of rest. For the past several decades we had hosted special holiday events, an activity that we took over when Mary's parents were no longer able. The large crowds on Memorial Day and Christmas in particular were very difficult for Mary although everyone pitched in to help. One requirement that I had established was that when dinner was over, Mary was to go in and relax and the men would clean up. That tradition continues in our children's homes. It's fair to say that we benefited greatly from the automatic dish washer installed in our kitchen.

Although this was not our first dish washer it was a far cry from the first patented dishwasher which was built by Joel Houghton in 1850 which was a wooden machine that had a hand-turned wheel that splashed water on the dirty dishes and did little to make them clean. A modification in 1865 by L.A. Alexander did little to improve the original concept. It utilized a hand crank and gearing to spin a rack of dirty dishes through the dishwater. A year later Josephine Cochrane who was the granddaughter of John Fitch (the inventor of the steamboat), declared, "If nobody else is going to invent a dishwasher, I'll do it myself." And do it she did.

She built wire compartments designed to fit cups, dishes and saucers. These compartments fit into a wheel that lays flat inside a copper boiler. A motor turns the wheel while hot soapy water squirted up from the boiler. She displayed her invention at the Chicago World's Fair in 1893. Like most appliances, the dishwasher has seen many improvements.

Even with her new Kenmore dishwasher, life was just becoming a chore rather than a pleasant experience for Mary, and frankly, caring for the large yard and painting and repairing the big house and the adjoining carriage house was beginning to wear heavily on me. Our children had long since left home and established themselves with their own families. We were proud of each of them. Nancy was a wonderful mother and housewife to Jim Ruane, with four children; one girl, Jaimie, and three sons, Cory, Kyle and Keean. They have four grandchildren (our great grandchildren) Alice, Gracie, Liam and McKenna. Our oldest son, Rich, is a Chemical Engineer who graduated from Juniata College and Drexel University and is employed by Merck Chemical. He married Jane Yoder who has recently retired from her teaching profession in the North Penn School system. She and Rich met at Juniata College. They have two children, Kate, who is doing missionary work in Brazil and of whom we ae very proud and Kevin, who is married to Chelsea and has a son, Noah.

Our next oldest son, George, married Carla Dawson and while they have no children, George is in charge of the voting machines for the County of Montgomery. Our youngest son, Rob, is a past Assistant District Attorney and a private attorney now. He graduated from Messiah College and got his Law Degree from Temple University. He has been married three times. Anna is his daughter from his first marriage with Linda, a second marriage with Ann produced no children and his present marriage to Priscilla Jane gave us our eighth grandchild, Julia.

We had a very good friend, Mary Davies, who lived at Fort Washington Estates and we determined to explore the possibility of joining her there. Of course we would have to sell our house first. I remembered that someone had at an earlier time mentioned that if ever we wanted to sell, they would like to be considered. I contacted them, told them what we wanted in price, and they agreed. We made application at Fort Washington Estates and were accepted.

There was a waiting list at Fort Washington and we wanted a two bedroom unit so the prospects didn't look too good for an imminent move, but we received a phone call indicating that a one bedroom unit was opening up. We went to look at it and though it was smaller than we had wanted, its location was most convenient and we said we would take it. We planned to move to a two bedroom unit when one opened up, but we became so adjusted to the one we were in, that we turned down a subsequent offer to relocate.

Downsizing is an experience that everyone should become familiar with because it happens to most of us, even if we only re-locate into a smaller house rather than a retirement community. The process begins with determining what you want take with you and measuring to make sure it will all fit into the new residence. Next you schedule an open house for the family, at which time everyone goes through and claims the items that they would like to have. Then a yard sale conducted with family member's assistance. The final step is an auction of items that seem to have value, but will no longer have a home, and the last step is a dumpster.

Moving day is a bit traumatic as is every change of environment and we approached it with some reservations. However, arrangements were made to have our first meal served in our new apartment and frankly, we never looked back. Mary Davies was a big help in expanding our acquaintances and because my Mary made friends so easily and was so well received by strangers, we became acclimated quickly. We found the concept that Rev. Coombs, Pastor of the Church of the Open Door, came up with to be most accommodating.

CHAPTER 9

ACTS RETIREMENT-LIFE COMMUNITIES FORT WASHINGTON ESTATES

One of the points of commonality among those involved in creating this story is that we are all residents by choice of Fort Washington Estates. The story of ACTS is in itself a memorable part of the past as well as an important part of the present and a promise for the future.

With a vision founded in faith, Pastor Coombs of the Church of the Open Door, with the help of members of his church set out to create a new and better way of living for retired church members.

Their idea was to provide a fulfilling and meaningful independent living lifestyle backed by a quality skilled health care environment that would be available should such care become necessary.

In a surprising coincidence, we discovered that a recently arrived new resident, Florence McDermott, had created a sketch based on information presented to her by a neighbor, Reginald Luff, in Hatboro, in order to facilitate initial fund raising.

Using their own talents and resources, Rev. Coombs and his congregation succeeded in building what is today known as Fort Washington Estates. It opened in 1972 and was so successful that another community was immediately planned to take care of the growing waiting list. The organization became a public corporation.

Today, ACTS Retirement- Life Communities is a 501©3 organization incorporated in the state of Pennsylvania with twenty-three life care retirement communities that are home to over 9000 seniors in eight states. Each of the ACTS facilities has a unique charm and character of its own, but all are governed by the same commitment to service, quality and care.

The mission statement of ACTS is as follows: "ACTS is committed to providing security and peace of mind to seniors by being a pre-eminent provider of retirement-life services, responsive to individual, social, personal, health and spiritual needs in a Christian atmosphere graced with loving-kindness, dignity, sensitivity, honesty and respect without prejudice or preference."

The choice of Fort Washington was the personal decision of each resident but we believe that all of ACTs facilities are wonderful. Mary and I personally experienced the service and care that we had come to expect from the caring staff and health care specialists that look after our well-being in this pioneer facility.

The word "independent" was foremost in our decision to make the move to Fort Washington. While activities are offered on a regular basis we have been completely free to decide whether or not to participate and free to go anywhere for any event we chose even though it might be located out in the complex world that we have come here to avoid in many cases.

Looming high on our list of service is the excellent food that is prepared by great chefs and served by wonderful high school youngsters who bring sunshine as well as food to our tables in the Susquehanna Room, a fancifully decorated dining room with table cloths and china where we have come to expect a wide selection of tasteful food presented in an appetizing fashion.

For the men perhaps the most persuasive factor is that grass cutting, painting and repairing appliances and burned out light bulbs is a thing of the past. Dedicated maintenance personnel are working daily to keep the grounds and household needs taken care of in a timely fashion. A simple request for service is promptly taken care of.

While not a regular daily service except when needed, the availability of health care when the need does arise, is an immeasurable asset and greatly appreciated by all residents. For those who have benefitted from the medical unit, the report of caring, professional assistance is reassuring.

For many, many years the image of an "old age home" was a negative one. For the most part the care was not personalized and often provided in an almost mystic environment. It was commonly looked upon as an act of putting someone away in a facility which provided minimum care and offered little opportunity for a satisfying lifestyle. This past image poses a serious problem for many facing the need to find answers to the increasing need for additional assistance. The vision of Rev. Coombs introduced an entirely new opportunity for couples or individuals who are facing the challenges of lost or reduced capabilities to find peace and a sense of making a difference in a fast moving society that has shown little or no patience with those who can no longer keep up the pace.

It also offered a chance for people facing the challenges of aging to provide a solution on their own without relying on the action of family members or putting the choices of how to face this challenge on their shoulders.

Fort Washington is the smallest of the ACTS as well as the oldest. Its smaller size offers a more intimate environment where everyone can get to know the other residents. A sense of extended family is a natural outgrowth of the experience while providing a much desired sense of fellowship.

Mary and I enjoyed more than a decade of relief from many of the external pressures of retirement. Our apartment afforded all the necessities we had become accustomed to in our three story house on Mattison Avenue in Ambler. We would no longer be able to accommodate the large dinner parties and family gatherings which had become a part of our routine, but other family members assumed those responsibilities and we were happy to help out where we could. It was wonderful to visit our timeshare properties with family members whenever we wished. All that we had to do was make the reservation, pack the car, leave word as to where we could be reached and take off. When we returned we unpacked and took up life where we had left off. There were no chores awaiting us.

Probably the only negative was the new relationships that we formed with other residents. Over the years, many that we had become very fond of, have passed on and the transition is not easy.

A little over ten years from the time that we had arrived in our new quarters, Mary began to show serious signs of a form of dementia and little by little she lost her ability to get about. We experienced a major change in our ability to travel and gradually to perform many of the daily things that we had always done. Mary was her usual uncomplaining self but it was sometimes necessary to try to interpret just what she could and couldn't do. At no time did she ever complain, meeting each day and new adjustment with a silent resilience and her customary smile.

The time finally came when she would have to remain in

Willow Brooke Court, the medical facility, because I could no longer take care of some of her daily requirements. We were able to work out a routine whereby she would sleep there and I would be able to get her in a wheel chair and we could be together during the day, returning in the evening. Family members visited and we even hosted a Christmas celebration with all of our immediate family in the small dining room.

I will be eternally grateful to the nursing staff and all of the nurse's aides who cared for her. They truly loved her and tenderly helped her through the difficult last days. They were most helpful and so understanding. Every member of our family shares this feeling of gratitude with me. Apart from the natural desire that it might all have turned out differently, we couldn't have asked for better treatment, both for Mary and for all of us.

Mary and I had sixty-two and a half wonderful years together and because of my faith, I know she is in a better place. I could not have asked for a better soul mate. My four children, their spouses and children and grandchildren all miss Mary very much but we all have a great deal to be thankful for in having loved her and been loved by her. Living in Fort Washington Estates has made it all easier.

Now the next phase of life at Fort Washington is working its way into my life. The support of the staff and the residents has certainly made my loss more bearable. There are many activities available to fill my lonely days and evenings. My family has been terrific, visiting, inviting, phoning and making certain that I am O.K. I look forward to whatever God has in mind for me in the remaining time that he grants me. I am thankful that it will be in the halls of Fort Washington Estates.

I have taken up the task of painting with acrylics, copying from pictures and photographs. My first attempt was to paint a photograph that I had taken from our outside door of the entrance to the Estates. It was a fall scene and the foliage was outstanding in color. For my first attempt I used water colors. The resulting painting was obviously not the greatest, but people recognized it and it had a certain color component all its own, which has become a major characteristic of all my work. I now paint almost a picture a week and post them on my door which many people claim to enjoy as they pass through in the hall. Another activity which consumes a considerable amount of my time is working on jigsaw puzzles. I have acquired somewhat of a reputation because of my ability to get them together in a relatively short period of time. I have come to philosophize jigsaw puzzles, comparing them to our lives. I picture Mary and I as the first two pieces of the grand picture of our lives. To that union each of us brought other combinations through our family relationships and the picture grows with each new addition as we build upon the original uniting of our lives. Each person in our lives becomes a piece of the final result as we live out the lives that God has planned for us.

We learn patience as we assemble our jigsaw puzzles, a trait that serves us well as we live out our lives. We also practice another good habit, that of perseverance. These two characteristics enable us to meet many of the challenges which seem to occur more frequently as we grow older.

Staying involved in the Fort Washington community eases the loss of Mary and makes life without her more bearable, although nothing could ever replace her. And of course family relationships continue to fill many pleasant hours. And I continue to remain active on the Board at Montgomery County Senior Adult Activities Center. There is so much for which to be grateful.

CHAPTER 10

MEET SOME OF MY FRIENDS

One of the things that occurred to me as I began to write down my thoughts on my past, was 'that there is a whole community of people who have shared many of the same experiences but have also had adventures totally foreign to me, living right here in Fort Washington Estates. It seemed a logical next step to include them in my reminiscing and so I asked for volunteers and was pleased to have had many respondents. I have often heard that it is not the building that makes a church great, but rather the people who populate it. I believe that is true of a retirement center and it is my privilege to introduce you to a cross-section of my friends here at Fort Washington Estates.

Harry E. Broadbent Jr.

Retired Navy Commander Harry Broadbent first set sail in Philadelphia, PA, on Jul 13th of 1922 when he was born to Harry Sr. and Elizabeth Ischi Broadbent, with God as his navigator. His only sibling, John W., was born two years later. The family resided in The Olney section of the city in a six-room row house. During the depression his father had to work two jobs and refinance their home in order to make out financially. Harry attended Olney High School where he was class president and graduated in 1940. He later learned that a fellow resident at Fort Washington Estates, Lorraine Kelso, had been a member of his class.

Harry then entered Drexel Institute of Technology (now Drexel University) and it was while in a fraternity house on campus that he heard the news of the Japanese attack on Pearl Harbor. He decided to enlist and reported to the enlistment center in Philadelphia. He noted a sign pointing to "Navy" and followed the sign, an action that literally changed his future and was directed by God, at least in Harry' s mind as he looks back upon the events that followed.

The sign in the lobby actually pointed to recruitment for the Naval Reserve and he signed up and he was stationed in Cape May, NJ, where he served on a mine sweeper, He successfully applied to be appointed to the U.S. Merchant Marine Academy located in Kings Point, Long Island, New York. He chose to be an engineering midshipman in order to get an earlier appointment. Part of his training was in the engine room of a merchant ship that made two trips to England during the time when the German "Wolf Pack" submarines were active in the Atlantic Ocean.

Upon graduating he received a Navy commission and marine engineering license. He finished his active service as an engineering officer on an attack transport in the Pacific. On release from active duty he remained in the Naval Reserve.

During the Korean War he was in a Submarine Reserve Unit, but not called for active duty and in the Vietnam War remained in reserve, but assigned to the Industrial Manager's Office in San Juan, Puerto Rico.

In civilian life, Harry raised four children, Susan, Harry III (Chuck), David and Barbara, with his first wife, Elizabeth

Taylor, in Glenside, PA. Upon returning to Drexel he switched from the business college to the engineering college and received his Mechanical Engineering degree in 1948. He was employed by the Atlantic Refining Company (ARCO) for twenty-three years. He next worked with the American Welding Society in Miami, Florida for another seventeen years. His combined military service consumed twenty-seven years.

He has a total of five grandchildren: Chad and Brian Bowman, Justin and Kim Broadbent, and Scott Josuweit. They have presented him with seven great grandchildren: Blake, Lance, Grant, William, Ben, John Paul and Charlotte.

After losing his first wife, Harry feels that God was at work once again. When he learned that there was going to be a cruise ship leaving from the Port of Philadelphia, he wanted to check it out so he made a reservation. He was asked by the man who leased the ship for the cruise to join a small group for cocktails and nightly dinners at the staff captain's table.

Dancing was a part of Harry's social routine, but he had never learned to jitterbug and wanted to accomplish that, so he signed up for a dance class aboard ship. The instructor was the featured dancer of the special entertainment group available on cruise ships and while she classified jitter bugging as swing dancing, it looked the same and Harry enjoyed the lessons. He also enjoyed her company. He learned that she was employed as a teacher of secretarial subjects in a Junior College as well as teaching adult education classes in a local public school and that her appearance on the cruise ship was just a summer assignment.

Harry was encouraged to find a guest for the group dinners and he approached Shirley Pulver, his dance instructor. She accepted the invitation and while the two did continue to see each other and to dance when possible, once the ship docked Harry did not expect to see Shirley again. However, not too much later he received a phone call saying that Shirley was doing a show in New Hampshire and she would be passing through Philadelphia on her way north from her home in Florida and she wondered if he could get the shipboard group together again. Somehow Harry worked it out

Harry spent a week's vacation in New Hampshire to see the show and made numerous trips to visit her in Fort Lauderdale over the next two years in addition to keeping in touch by exchanging many letters and phone calls. The two were married in 1970 and set up housekeeping in Fort Lauderdale where they lived for the next forty-one years before coming north and taking up residence in Fort Washington Estates. As a result of his marriage to Shirley, he gained an additional son, Loran Pulver, and two more granddaughters. She has subsequently passed and Harry is now stationed in Willow Brooke Court where he is receiving treatment for a broken hip and other physical difficulties, but taking active part in many of the special programs offered there.

PAIGE C. KERR

Paige C. Kerr was born in 1928 in the hospital in Chester, Pa. She had one sister, Geraldine, who died shortly after her birth. Paige attended both grade school and high school in the Media School District, before going on to the University of Pennsylvania in Philadelphia, from which she graduated with a degree in English, majoring in journalism.

Growing up in Media, which was comparatively unsettled at that time, Paige, like most people of the depression era, was poor, but didn't recognize it. She remembers hearing about the attack on Pearl Harbor, but had to ask where it was located. During WWII she was in college and suffered like everyone else from gas rationing and shortages of many items.

She met Henry Stephen Kerr, Jr. (Steve) on a pre-arranged blind date. Steve was born in Philadelphia, attended Olney High School and went to Drexel University. They had two children, Henry Stephen III and Marianne Kerr Nolan and have one grandchild, Elizabeth Grace Nolan who is presently attending a college in Indiana. They settled in a house in Flourtown, then moved to a larger house in Fort Washington, both of which are located northeast of Philadelphia, PA. From here they entered Fort Washington Estates, a branch of ACTS Retirement – Life Community in 2001.

Paige worked with Curtis Publishing Company in Philadelpia in Public Relations and later became an associate editor of "Jack and Jill" magazine. Her husband was in the construction business. They particularly enjoyed travelling by train to the National Parks scattered throughout the United States and visited most of them. They also journeyed by air to England, Scotland and Wales. Cape May, NJ was their favorite vacation spot. Both she and her husband enjoyed classical music and were thrilled to change over to television.

Steve is deceased and Paige is living in the Assisted Living unit of Fort Washington Estates known as Oak Ridge Terrace.

Donna Marie Wolfe King

Tulsa, Oklahoma seems like a long way off and for Donna King it is because that's where she has to go to return to her birth place and visit her family. On May 2 of 1926 she was born to Donna Hayden Wolfe and Andrew J. Wolfe. The oldest of three daughters, she had two sisters, Helen Garrott and Ann Wolfe Lyda (who passed on five years ago). Donna attended kindergarten through high school in Tulsa, but after graduating from high school she journeyed to Dallas, Texas to attend Southern Methodist University.

Donna, being the oldest, had a very special relationship with her grandparents (Mary and Ross Hayden), whom she just adored. She stayed with them while she was in SMU. She and her sisters had ridden their bikes to visit their grandmother as they were growing up in Tulsa. When she moved to Dallas, each of the sisters spent a month over the summer with their grandparents. Donna credits her Grandmother for establishing a firm religious foundation in her which has served her well through the years. And she is especially grateful for the hints that she received in her grandmother's kitchen.

While she was in college a classmate suggested that she join her on a date with a friend of her boyfriend, but the episode was more complicated than that. Initially Clare and Jodi, two of Donna's classmates had been out with two soldiers from Camp Maxie. Jodi was not impressed with her date so Clare made another date with her boyfriend but requested a substitute for the guy that Jodi had dated. The arrangements were made, but Jodi couldn't make the date and Clare asked Donna to go in her place. Donna at first said no, but when Clare couldn't find anyone else, she agreed to go.

She believes it was providential that all this happened, because that was how she met her future husband, Charles King. Camp Maxie was not far from the college. They dated regularly before Charlie was sent overseas and subsequently saw action in the Battle of the Bulge in Belgium. She was only 15 years old when the Japanese attacked Pearl Harbor and while she remembers the announcement of President Roosevelt declaring war on Japan, suddenly she was in the middle of the conflict and writing daily letters to the man with whom she had fallen in love.

Charlie was from Ambler, PA. His folks, Dorothy Betz and Frank J. King operated a grocery store in the small town of Ambler. "King and Betz" was a popular attraction, but it faced many challenges during WWII because of the short supply of many items which led to the rationing of gasoline, sugar and butter. The King family was quite large with thirteen children in addition to the parents. Charlie was the second oldest.

When Charlie returned home from overseas, the two were married and they made the trip north where she was somewhat overwhelmed by the size of her new family. She and Charlie had a room on Fairview Avenue during that first summer, but they ate their meals with the King family. Donna recalls being told by her husband, "When there is a seat at the table, grab it." There wasn't room enough for everyone to sit down at the same time. She remembers also that all summer long the men were involved playing baseball and then hashing over the game afterward. It was very frustrating for a twenty year old young bride who had left her home in Oklahoma and was having difficulty making adjustments in her new environment. To make matters worse her sister Helen contracted polio and almost died.

That fall they were able to find an apartment on the third floor of a building on Euclid Avenue which was characterized by excessive heat in the summer and a lack of heat in the winter. Two years later they were able to rent a two bedroom apartment in the Manor House on Forest Avenue and after another seven years, bought their first home, a Cape Cod on Belmont Avenue where they remained for six years. They next purchased a three story house on Euclid Avenue and finally found the house of their dreams, back once again on Belmont Avenue, a Cape Cod which Donna really hated to leave, but after Charlie succumbed to dementia, she decided to enter Fort Washington Estates, a retirement community in nearby Upper Dublin Township.

The couple had two children, Linda Anne King Nyman and Gary Andrew King. Donna began teaching when Gary was ten. Donna took a position as a Kindergarten teacher in the Mattison Avenue School in the Ambler School District, joining a distinguished cadre of elementary school teachers who became her long- time friends. Frances Behringer, the other Kindergarten teacher, was a fabulous woman from whom Donna believes she learned more about teaching than she had ever learned in college. Mrs. Behringer had been her husband's first grade teacher when he went to the Mattison Avenue School as a child. Charlie always joked that if he had had a better start, he might have become President of the United States. The Ambler School District merged with Whitpain and Lower Gwynedd to form the Wissahickon School district.

Donna had to get extra credits in order to get her teaching certificate in Pennsylvania and so she studied Latin at Gwynedd Mercy College in Gwynedd, PA, on top of her classroom duties. She additionally took a correspondence course in Geography from Southern Methodist University with a little help from Charlie. She enjoyed her teaching experience so much that she claimed she would have done it without pay (except that Charlie objected strenuously to that idea). She reluctantly retired after 25 years, but then began teaching a Nursery School class at her church, First Presbyterian Church of Ambler, for several more years.

Her husband was active in real estate and insurance, working first with the H.C. Biddle Company where he had worked before going into the service and finally the J.A. Cassidy Co. He was active for many years in the Ambler Kiwanis Club and served as Secretary for decades.

Donna has three grandchildren: Amanda Leflar Harris, Casey Leflar and Christopher King. She also has six great grandchildren: Maya and Emmie Harris, Finnegan and Shamus Leflar, and Kalie and Cara King.

Returning home to Tulsa was a difficult task and it was

usually accomplished by air plane, but she and Charlie did drive it occasionally. Most of their travel was by automobile, but they did enjoy vacationing, journeying to Florida, the Finger Lakes of New York State and also to Bermuda, Jamaica, Hawaii, the Canadian Rockies and a cruise in the Caribbean.

Eating out was difficult with the family and the busy schedule, but special meals like Kiwanis and various teachers' dinners were regular events which they tried to attend. Donna enjoyed entertaining and often had friends over for dinner. The coming of television was a thrill, replacing the rather dull experience of listening to the radio. Movies always held a special charm for Donna which she continues to enjoy on Monday evenings in the auditorium at Fort Washington Estates. She also enjoys live theater and musical productions.

Nancy H. Lange

Nancy Lange was born at Geisinger Hospital in Danville, PA, but her family lived in nearby Lewisburg. Nancy had two older sisters, Bette and Frances. Her parents, Anne and Frank Hitchcock, lived on Market Street in Lewisburg, next to her father's office. He was a doctor of the old school who was on call twenty-four hours a day, seven days a week, and three hundred sixty-five days a year. During the depression her father was often paid with chickens, eggs, venison, or whatever the patient was able to come up with in payment.

Dr. Hitchcock was so committed to his profession that he never took a vacation. In 1939 one of his patients offered him the use of the family's cottage on Lake Clear located about nine miles from Saranac Lake across from Mt. Regis Mountain in the Adirondack Mountains of New York State. The doctor drove the family to the site on a Saturday but returned back to his work on Sunday While there, a seaplane made a landing on the lake and taxied to a nearby wharf. The pilot asked Nancy's mother if the children could take a ride with him in the plane and she gave her permission. The flight over the scenic area was a memorable experience for the young girls.

Another memory in growing up was a special relationship which developed between Nancy and an older couple who lived on the other side of Market Street. They were referred to as "Aunt and Uncle". He was a book salesman and often invited Nancy to visit while he read to her. He would trace his progress in reading with his finger while she was seated on his lap. She followed his finger with her eyes as it moved from word to word. She actually learned to read from this experience which was a big help since there was no kindergarten in those days and she started school in the first grade. Nancy attended school from the first grade through college in Lewisburg. She did however skip the sixth grade along with eight other of her fellow students. While a junior in high school, Nancy played the clarinet. Since the school did not have a football team or large athletic field, marching practice took place on the streets of Lewisburg. Rehearsals began at 7:30 in the morning and even so, the residents enjoyed the music.

Nancy remembers that she was studying when her mother came into her room to tell her of the attack at Pearl Harbor. "This means war," her mother said. At first Nancy experienced a feeling of excitement, but it didn't last long, During World War II she remembers collecting tin cans, newspapers and soda bottles. She also recalls ration stamps for gasoline, meat and sugar.

Saturday afternoons were usually spent in the movies and she went on her first date at age 6 which featured a movie show and followed with a Hershey popsicle with the potential of finding an offer of a second one "free", printed on the stick. Her mother was famous for her roasts, but there were occasional trips out on Sunday for dinner after church. Prices were a bit different in her younger days. Bread was only 10 cents a loaf, a can of tomato soup cost a dime and the movies were ten cents for a short while, but then a one cent tax was added.

In June of 1945, Nancy's sister Frances was getting married to a member of the United States Air Force in Boca Raton. Nancy, her father and mother, and an aunt accompanied Frances on a train trip to Florida with a stop in Washington, D.C. which allowed a short time for sight-seeing because of connections. The train ride also exposed evidence of racial segregation in the south as the train made its way through the rural county side.

After the wedding, Nancy and her family went to a restaurant for dinner. During dinner, her father became agitated and began clutching his chest. He asked Nancy to go back to the hotel to get his Nitro Glycerin. She ran all the way and because the elevator was tied up, ran up the four flights only to realize that she did not have a key to get in. When she returned to the lobby, her family was just entering. They had called a cab and they took the elevator up to their room where her mother called for a doctor. He determined that her father should go to the hospital and an ambulance was called. Unfortunately, he died on the elevator. With today's ability to deal with heart attacks, especially the trained response on the part of the emergency responders, the doctor would most likely have survived.

Nancy worked after school at a bookstore. She also did a lot of babysitting. She was able to get financial assistance to attend Bucknell College from which she graduated in 1950 with a Bachelor of Science Degree in Commerce and Finance with a major in Secretarial Science.

Her husband, Norman, was born in Braintree, MA and

the two met at Eagles Mere Resort where she was working as a waitress and he as a bus boy. He was a foreman for US Rubber Company, eventually concluding his career as a Management Consultant with Hay Associates. After graduation Nancy did secretarial work until her babies arrived and then she was a full-time mother. Once the children were grown she returned to work at the Spring House Corporation, a publishing house.

After six years there, Nancy asked for something more challenging. Two weeks later she was offered a position as Medical Librarian. She would be following a woman who had her Master's in Library

Sciences. She re-entered the educational program and earned a Master's degree in Library Science (Informational Studies) from Drexel Institute.

She and her husband had four children. David is married to Julie and they have two children, Nate and Ben. Lisa (who died at age 46 of Ovarian Cancer) was married to John with no children. Heidi is married to Roy with children, Emily and Colleen and Richard, married to Holly has two children, Brandon and Summer.

In 2012, Nancy decided to enter Fort Washington Estates, the first of dozens of ACTS Life-Retirement Services which dot the eastern United States all the way to Florida. Like all of her activities, she has plunged into several roles including singing in the resident Choraliers group, making public announcements in the dining hall at the evening meal on Wednesdays and calling bingo for the residents on Friday evenings.

SARAH MURPHY

Charleroi, Pennsylvania was in the throes of the depression when banker Ross Allen and his wife, Marie, welcomed their second daughter into the world. Quadruplets (four boys) had been born before Sarah but the babies lived only a few days or weeks. The steel mills and the bituminous coal mines had pretty much shut down. Fortunately the bank where her father worked was the only one of three that did not close. Money was tight, but being thrifty (canning fruit and vegetables), they managed to get by.

The town of Charleroi was located on the Monongahela River, about thirty miles south of Pittsburgh. The main industry in town was the manufacturing of glass (Corning), but across the river was a huge steel plant and there were many coal mines around. There was much pollution in the area. Sarah remembers coming in from playing and she would be black from the soft coal dust (soot). She said the area was almost 75% first generation immigrants, mostly from Europe, and also blacks from the South. She further remembers looking across the Monongahela and seeing crosses burning on the hillside as the Ku Klux Klan went about its work of hatred.

Sarah's older sister suffered from epileptic seizures and because of the times she was shunned. Other children didn't understand when she had a grand-mal and were afraid. To make matters worse, their mother died when Sarah was only thirteen. Her life was changed from this point on. Sarah, as did most children during this era, played jacks, hop scotch, paper dolls and belonged to the Girl Scouts. Most children of this era used their imagination and made do with toys that were simple and without the detailed structure of today's children's toys. She also clearly recalls having hobos eating in her kitchen. It seems that these traveling individuals somehow marked the homes of people who were receptive and gracious, and they would make repeat calls and also spread the word to other travelers.

During the mid – thirties the family journeyed to New

Mexico to visit an aunt and uncle. The aunt had infantile paralysis so they had moved to that area for her health. Sarah's mother cashed in her teacher's pension and another aunt accompanied them to help cover expenses. The trip was made during the dust storm era, driving was difficult, but they saw many of the national parks. It was a memorable experience for a seven year old.

After graduating from high school, Sarah headed for Philadelphia to begin her college education at Drexel Institute, now Drexel University. College life in those days was a bit different from today. Dormitories were segregated and were either men's or women's dorms. There was only one telephone on each floor and it was usually busy. Cell phones did not exist. There was a woman in charge of the dorm and strict regulations controlled the time to get in during the evenings. There were no large parking lots because few students had an automobile.

It was here that Sarah met her husband to be. Robert, a returning Navy veteran, was a year ahead of her, graduating in 1950. She followed in 1951 and both received Bachelor of Science Degrees. After they were married they settled in an apartment in West Oak Lane. They had three children-- Dennis, Ellen and Ann. In 1954 they moved to Warrington Township and this became their permanent residence until Bob's passing in 2011. Sarah was a member of the Warrington Junior Women's Club, served as the Secretary to the Township School Board and was a member of the Warrington Historical Society.

Bob was a member of the Lion's Club (President one year) and served on several Township boards. After his retirement he served as a member of the Bucks County Community College Authority Board. His career was with National Cash Register. He served as Business Manager of the Palisades

School District and was in the Administration of the Buck's County Community College.

Sarah worked for the Goodyear Tire and Rubber Company in Philadelphia until Dennis was born and later, when the children were in school, she went to work for Engineering & Planning Co. and then for the Carroll Engineering Corp. Both of the later were located in Warrington, PA.

The Murphys travelled every year, making three trips to Europe, one of which involved seeing the continent by rail. This trip included one day on the Oriental Express. They also visited Alaska, Canada, Nova Scotia and covered most of the United States, which included three trips to California. Some winters they escaped the cold blasts by going to the balmy sunshine of Florida. Because of their love for history they also visited Revolutionary and Civil War locations.

When at home, they enjoyed reading, entertaining friends, movies and every year Sarah and sometimes Bob would go to New York for a Broadway Show. They also liked to dine occasionally at a Bucks County Inn. Organic gardening was both Bob's and Sarah's hobby so they always had flowers and fresh veggies including tomatoes, corn and potatoes.

Bob and Sarah were a close family and the entire family was together on Thanksgiving Day of 2011 to celebrate Bob's memory, for he had died in August of that year. All three children, their spouses and nine grandchildren were there.

ROSA NEFF

Rosa Neff was born in the Tioga area of Philadelphia. Her parents, John and Bertha Neff were both German and didn't speak English. She found it difficult in school because she didn't speak English either. With the help of first and second grade teachers who tutored both she and her mother, Rosa overcame that difficulty and studied Business and Library Science at Temple University. She also attended Bible College for four years and trained as a nurse at St. Luke's hospital in Philadelphia.

She grew up in a row house in Philadelphia and remembers eating soup every day. She later occupied a Ranch House in Roslyn, PA for forty-four years. She was active in her church and spent 20 years connected to Pioneer girls and 50 years with the girl Scouts of America. During WWII she was an errand messenger by bicycle for the neighborhood Air Raid Wardens.

She served eight years in the United States Marine Reserve and three years in the Coast Guard Reserve. She then spent fifty-seven years in the Coast Guard Auxiliary and remained active as a Training Officer until her passing. She also made many mission trips with church groups to Haiti, Peru, Holland and Brazil.

She was employed at Merck for thirty-eight years at their plant in West Point and a Travel Consultant for fifteen years with the Willow Grove Travel Agency. Rosa has cruised on a hundred and fifty ships and traveled throughout the United States by automobile and rail.

In 2006 she entered Fort Washington Estates, the first of ACTS Retirement-Life Communities, with her friend of fifty-seven years, Alice Drew, who predeceased her. Rosa immediately began volunteer work, writing for the newsletter and working in the medical unit at Willow Brooke Court. She has recently gone to join Alice.

Helen Ernestine Alsup Schotsch

On March 4 1921, Robert Alsup and his wife, Erna Schuhmann Alsup welcomed a daughter, Helen Ernestine into their family and into their home in Kopperl, Texas, a small town near Dallas Fort Worth. The family grew to include two brothers and one sister and Ernestine by-passed her first name and was called, "Ernestine. The family moved about a good bit, spending some time in Bledsoe, Texas then relocating into Hobbs, New Mexico, which Ernestine recalls as being in the dust bowl. In 1933, during the depression, most of her summer found her running about barefooted, dodging tumble weeds and trying to escape the dust that constantly filled the air. She can also vividly remember sitting at the kitchen table reading by a kerosene lamp and later being really excited to have gas lights hanging in the center of the rooms throughout the house. She spent later summers in Girl Scout or Church camps in the mountains of New Mexico.

She recalls coming home from church on December 7, 1941, and hearing of the attack on Pearl Harbor. Also, her first boyfriend was in the 200th Coast Artillery Unit in the Pacific, taken prisoner by the Japanese and his being involved in the Bataan Death March. Fortunately he survived and came back home in 1945, but he had been in prison for four or five years.

Ernestine attended ten years in the Hobbs' District schools. In 1937 and 1938, she borrowed her mother's Kodak camera to take all of the Hobbs' High School yearbook pictures for the year book of which she was the editor. She then went to the Eastern New Mexico Junior College for one year before going on to earn a Bachelor of Science Degree from the University of New Mexico in Albuquerque, New Mexico. She continued on with graduate studies at Carnegie Mellon and the University of Pittsburgh after relocating in the city of smog after her marriage to Joseph George Schotsch on Dec.26, 1945.

She and Joe had met in a Conga line at a USO Center in Albuquerque. They spent their honeymoon in the trip to Pittsburgh from New Mexico. They have four children (all boys): Robert, Kenneth, James and Timothy. They also have six grandchildren: Casandra, Timothy, Tyler, Kadye, Trevor and Emma. As of February of 2013 they have two great grandchildren; Alyssa and Kalee.

Ernestine began her years of employment teaching for two years in Carrizozo, New Mexico, which is close to White Sands where the atomic bomb tests were made. She spent another year and a half in Albuquerque and finished up her teaching career with a stretch of eighteen years in the School District of Pittsburgh, PA. Joe began his employment career at Ditto Inc. (a duplicating company) and then with Bell & Howell.

Looking back, she can remember when bread was only 5 cents a loaf, 5 pounds of potatoes cost 25 cents and bananas were only 10 cents a pound. Eating out only happened on rare occasions when Dad took Mom and the four children out to dinner. One such occasion did take place when the family went to a cafeteria in Lubbock, Texas, in 1935. It was not until 1970 that she owned a portable dishwasher and their microwave arrived in 1975.

From 1946 to 1993 the family traveled by automobile. Before that there was precious little travel of any sort. A rare trip saw Ernestine and Joe en route to visit the Alsup folks in New Mexico, but later air travel became possible and trips became more frequent. They also availed themselves of the opportunity to visit Alaska, Israel, Sweden and England. For entertainment, card games were the main event. Then television opened new venues.

Ernestine came to Fort Washington Estates on June 22, 2006. She chose this location because of its proximity to her son's home in Chestnut Hill, PA. She has been very active in the Resident's Association, serving as President for a couple of terms.

RUTH SMITH

Ruth Smith was born to George and Bertha Egerter in Kensington Women's Hospital in Philadelphia, PA on the nineteenth of November in the year 1929.

Her brother, George Jr. was born in 1932.

Ruth attended Wright Elementary School, located a block from her home. She next attended Gillespie Junior High and went on to Germantown High School before graduating from Temple University in 1951 with a degree in Elementary Education. Her former High School would have celebrated its 100th Anniversary in 2014 had it not closed its doors.

She enjoyed school and learning. While other children were busy with other activities, she was hard at work with her books. Learning new things has always held a major spot on her "to do" list. She spent thirty-two years teaching in the Philadelphia School System and after retirement, volunteered in the "Art Goes to School Program" for an additional twenty-two years and a like number of years working with the Museum at the University of Pennsylvania where she served as a Mobil Guide.

The Art Goes to School Program is an organization located with many chapters in the Delaware Valley who research art work and make presentations in schools. At the University of Pennsylvania she was part of group which varied from 20-30 people, representing a mixture of religions, race and nationalities with meetings about three times a year. As a Mobil Guide, she also took certain relics from the museum to the schools from the Egyptian, Early American and African cultures.

In both of these volunteer positions she worked with children in the elementary school level, sharing the values of the works of art and the mysteries of artifacts from the museum with the children.

Ruth lost her husband, John Baird, when he was only 38 years of age. He was employed as a chemist at Rohm & Haas. In time she met Robert Smith and they were wed. Robert was employed as an Electronic Engineer at RCA which subsequently became a part of General Electric. They were wed for 33 years.

Ruth's uncle, Bill Roehl, was like a father to her. He had built a house in Harvey Cedars on Long Beach Island in New Jersey which became a vacation home for Ruth and her family. He was an avid fisherman and she still has many of his records of catches including dates, time of day, weather conditions and tides.

Ruth's daughter, Linda, and three grandchildren, Brian, Richard and Amy continue to visit the shore each summer, enjoying the beach, boating and swimming in the ocean and the bay.

In 1965 Ruth settled in Oreland where she spent a great deal of her spare time in the garden. She still has a couple of jars of tomatoes and jams made from cherries, plums, grapes and apples grown on the property which she had canned during her more active days.

Looking back Ruth recalls hearing of the attack on Pearl Harbor on the radio, and being shocked at the news. She also remembers writing to a service man who was killed in action during WWII along with the rationing of gasoline and sugar that characterized those dark days.

More pleasant memories include eight trips to Europe and visits to Alaska, Hawaii, Costa Rico and Florida. The family also travelled to several National Parks and other western sites in the United States. After the death of Robert, she decided to look for a retirement community and although she and Bob had discussed Spring House Estates (primarily because it offered a workshop) Ruth wound up at Fort Washington

Estates, another of AC TS Life- Retirement Communities in 2011. Summing things up, Ruth said, "Aging doesn't really sink in, until it happens to you."

Carole Zacharias

A march of a thousand miles begins with a single step." That's an old Chinese proverb and in a sense, the first step for Carole Louise Baron Zacharias took place when her mother, Louise Beck gave birth to her in Jefferson Hospital in Philadelphia, Pennsylvania, on November 27th of 1944. Carole had no siblings. She was raised by her grandparents, Frank and Louise Beck, in a twin house located on Township Line Road in Cheltenham, PA. She attended Rowand Elementary School, Shoemaker Elementary School, the Elkins Park Junior High School and Cheltenham High School from which she graduated in1962.

Carole met her future husband, Albert Zacharias, while visiting with friends at Temple University where he was studying. They were married in 1965 and set up housekeeping in an apartment in Philadelphia. They have one daughter named Joanne. Albert joined the military and the couple moved around a good bit, moving first to Wichita Falls, Texas, then to Summerville, South Carolina, and subsequently to Landover, Maryland. Carole remembers being surprised at the amount of racial segregation that still existed in the south at the time. When Albert was sent to Vietnam, Carole returned to an apartment in Willow Grove.

Carole's daughter, Joanne, married David Torillo and is the mother of Nicole, Louise and Anthony John, who goes by the nickname A.J., making Carole a proud grandmother.

After graduating from Cheltenham High School, Carole attended Pierce Business School in Philadelphia and was employed by Horn & Hardart Baking Company as a keypunch operator from 1963 to 1967. Although she was an ardent supporter of the Horn & Hardart automat, there was no direct connection with her employment, Wages at that time were notably low and she earned only $45 a week. Her frugal grandmother insisted that she put some of that in the bank and she was left with little money for her own expenses after carfare and lunches were paid.

She also worked as a laboratory secretary and receptionist. in Prince George's County Hospital in Maryland from 1970 to1972. Her final place of employment was the Abington Hospital where she served from 1972 until 2008. Abington assisted her in attending Gwynedd Mercy College to earn a degree in Health Information Management in 1992. She became a Systems Analyst in the hospital IT Department until a spinal condition caused her to retire.

Experience in the Vietnam conflict caused serious changes in the character of her husband and the two were unable to solve their difficulties and parted ways. Carole devoted much of her time and effort to taking care of her elderly grandparents. After their passing, she moved back into the house on Township Line Road in Cheltenham where she had been raised as a child, spending thirty-three years of her life there. Recognizing the reality of her health condition and not wanting to become a burden to her daughter, Carole made the decision to sell the house and enter the retirement community at Fort Washington Estates, a part of ACTS Retirement – Life Communities, Inc. which operates fourteen sites throughout the eastern part of the United States.

Probably the most important event in her past was the Vietnam War because it resulted in the destruction of her marriage through its impact on her husband. As a result, she became involved in protesting the war publicly. Whatever one might have felt about that conflict, there is no question that the effort was frustrating because there seemed to be no solution and no real determination to end it. It was difficult for our troops to determine who the enemy was, and often an extreme effort was made to take a hill or fortification, only to pull out and abandon that site. Past wars featured the taking of a hill or a city and moving forward to the next target until the enemy surrendered, but Vietnam offered no apparent solution and the consequences on our fighting forces was extreme and often resulted in character changes resulting in catastrophic results such as Carole's destroyed family.

As a Fort Washington resident, she has participated in a project designed to share memories of activities from the past. While she has no recollection of activities that took place during the second world war because of her age, she was certainly aware of the Korean War and in fact, remembers that a next-door neighbor was enlisted to be engaged in that conflict.

She greatly enjoyed vacationing in Alaska, Germany and Italy. Her trip to Alaska was a combination of cruising and a train trip which she enjoyed very much. If living expenses there were not so expensive and she was in better physical condition and younger, she would have probably seriously considered moving there. One tempting feature is that the ratio of men to women is ten men to every woman. She indicates that there is a quotation that says, "the odds are great, but the results are odd."

She saw humpback whales, "calving" of the glaciers in Glacier Bay (large portions of the glacier falling off into the water), seals lying on floating cakes of ice, and her group visited a salmon hatchery where they saw tiny salmon which would eventually be released into the wider waterways. They even tried their luck panning for gold.

Carole presently is serving her fourth year as President of the Resident's Association at Fort Washington. She also keeps busy with many volunteer responsibilities.

MY CONCLUSIONS

My first conclusion is that I have really appreciated the opportunity to interact with the wonderful people at Fort Washington Estates and I thank God for each of them. My comments herein reflect my basic understanding of life. I've read a lot of philosophic explanations of life in general and history in particular. From all of this information and including my own personal experience I would like to attempt to put on paper the conclusions about many things according to my learning, my experience and my beliefs.

When I started this work I referenced the Bible with the famous quote, "In the beginning." That is where I want to start this conclusion because my belief about the beginning of the world influences much of what I have ultimately concluded. I cannot seriously consider anything that I observe without believing wholeheartedly that a supreme being created the wonderful, fully coordinated world into which I was born.

Any study of the body in which I have spent the last ninety-one years is terribly complex, but every part of it plays a definite role in my existence. Any thought that something so remarkable could be the result of some freak accident is preposterous and totally unacceptable in my mind. The existence of God certainly relies upon a leap in faith, but to deny him is a leap in incredulity.

I believe that over the centuries God has unveiled some of His secrets to mankind. I cannot begin to understand the inner workings of the Creator, but I continue to see evidence of His wisdom and foresight. Wise people have explained to me the reason that He gave us free choice that involves a relationship of love. He wants us to follow His teachings because we love Him, not because we fear Him or because we have been programed to do so.

I have some other problems with how things are run, but I realize that from a human's standpoint, my view is very self-centered and limited. For instance, I have real problems with the suffering that takes place. But I have learned to put my faith completely in Him and to trust that, because He loves us, His will controls the ultimate outcome.

Prayer is another difficult thing to understand. How could each individual's thoughts and wishes be known to God and how can He hear our prayers? I strongly believe that an answer to that is visible every day in our lives today. How can anyone transmit tiny dots throughout the world that are received on a screen and form images and transmit sound such as happens with our television sets? To me, this makes transmission of our thoughts to one who has the ability to create a complex universe is duck soup.

How does one transfer all of that ideology into our daily life? First and foremost, if God created us, He must have had a reason for our life and we should live our lives to constantly seek His guidance and support. I have no difficulty looking back over my life to find evidence of divine guidance. The circumstances which made possible my finding and ultimately marrying Mary is proof positive, but throughout my life I have been privileged to accomplish things for which I frankly was not equipped, but with God's help and guidance the outcome has been very satisfying to me and I hope to Him.

My political views are similarly based upon my belief in God. I believe that government, like God, should be a framework within which we live our lives and pursue the happiness expressed in the Declaration of Independence. I believe that we have been created with those unalienable rights and they are a gift from God and not from man. In that regard they become unalienable and remain a permanent right with which man must not interfere. Within the framework of government we are free to choose how we will live our life, whom we will chose as our life's partner, what we will choose as a profession, where we will live, etc.

I do believe that we should carefully make those decisions and base them upon the laws that God set forth in the Bible. The Ten Commandments were provided for the Israelites because they had been in slavery where their choices were limited and they needed special guidance for their lives when they had been set free. They were not given as suggestions, but rather as commandments to be followed faithfully. They are part of the framework established by God for His creation.

We need to understand that what we call morality is really a condition of obedience to God's rules. These commands cannot be thoughtlessly or selfishly rearranged by man in his so-called laws. I believe that God's laws are unchanged and unchangeable. They are to be the standard for our living. We are expected to be able to distinguish right from wrong and seek to do what is morally right. Because we are human and because we do have freedom to choose, man has established laws to help keep us in line and retain some form of order.

The book of Proverbs sets forth many specifics in terms of how we should attack the problems of life but they are in keeping with the Ten Commandments. The challenge is in keeping them. It is also important for the government which we have established to maintain the same standard of right and wrong when writing its laws, intended to supplement the dictates of God. The Bible describes the consequences of seeking to reach heaven in the story about the Tower of Babel. He introduced confusion by using foreign languages which ended communication. It is a message that He does not want us to seek equality or supremacy to Him, just as He made it clear to Adam and Eve. God is God and we are his creation, made is His image and likeness, but not His equal.

We are to look to Him for guidance and strength. The Bible is full of examples where circumstances indicated that He wanted man to look to Him for solutions in many cases. I believe that there is a difference between material things and spiritual things. Material things are destructible, spiritual things are indestructible. We are spiritual, living in a material body. Things happen to our bodies, finally resulting in death, but our spirit remains alive and will be given a new and different form. I believe that God has a plan for each of us. It is our task to seek to follow his leadings, but follow them or not, He will win out in the final analysis.

Finally, I can imagine a world where each of us seeks to follow His commands, with no breaking of the Ten Commandments and following His directive that the greatest of all commandments is to love Him and to love our fellow man as we love ourselves. There would be no theft, lying, lust, murders, bullying, nor any of the things which today find themselves into the news each day. I know that that's what lies ahead for us in heaven, wherever that may be.

The end

Printed in the United States
By Bookmasters